Three Authors of Alienation
Bombal, Onetti, Carpentier

Latin American Monographs, No. 36
Sponsored by the Institute of Latin American Studies
The University of Texas at Austin

Three
Authors
of
Alienation

BOMBAL, ONETTI, CARPENTIER

M. Ian Adams

UNIVERSITY OF TEXAS PRESS • AUSTIN AND LONDON

Grateful acknowledgment is made to the following sources for permission to use quotations and selections in this volume:

Juan Carlos Onetti, for quotations from *El pozo, Tan triste como ella, La vida breve, Juntacadáveres*, and *El astillero*, by Juan Carlos Onetti.

Editorial y Distribuidora "Orbe" Ltda., for quotations from *La última niebla*, by María Luisa Bombal.

Compañía General de Ediciones, S.A., for quotations from *Los pasos perdidos*, by Alejo Carpentier.

Holt, Rinehart and Winston, Inc., for quotations from *The Sane Society*, by Erich Fromm. Copyright © 1955 by Erich Fromm. Reprinted by permission of Holt, Rinehart and Winston, Inc.

Pantheon Books, A Division of Random House, Inc., for quotations from *The Divided Self*, by R. D. Laing, copyright 1969; and Tavistock Publications, Ltd., for selections from *The Divided Self*, by R. D. Laing.

Alice L. Kahler and George Braziller, Inc., for selections from *The Tower and the Abyss*, by Erich Kahler, copyright 1967.

Library of Congress Cataloging in Publication Data

Adams, Michael Ian, 1937–
    Three authors of alienation.

    (Latin American monographs; no. 36)
    Bibliography: p.
    Includes index.
    1. Bombal, María Luisa, 1910–   –Criticism and interpretation. 2. Onetti, Juan Carlos, 1909– –Criticism and interpretation. 3. Carpentier, Alejo, 1904–   –Criticism and interpretation. 4. Alienation (Social psychology) in literature. I. Texas. University at Austin. Institute of Latin American Studies. II. Title. III. Series: Latin American monographs (Austin, Tex.); no. 36.
PQ7081.A4   863   74–32397
ISBN 0–292–78009–5

THIS WORK
IS DEDICATED TO
T.J.D.,
WITH THANKS

CONTENTS

Acknowledgments   xi

1. General Aspects of Alienation   3

2. María Luisa Bombal: Alienation and the
   Poetic Image   15

3. Juan Carlos Onetti: Alienation and the
   Fragmented Image   37

4. Alejo Carpentier: Alienation, Culture, and Myth   81

5. Concluding Remarks   107

Notes   111

Selected Bibliography   115

Index   123

ACKNOWLEDGMENTS

I would like to thank Dr. Carlos Mellizo for his invaluable aid in revising the translations, and Dr. George D. Schade for his kindness, encouragements, and aid in the initial writing of the manuscript.

Three Authors of Alienation
Bombal, Onetti, Carpentier

1. General Aspects of Alienation

The intent of this work is to study alienation as a literary theme in the selected works of three contemporary Latin American authors: María Luisa Bombal, Juan Carlos Onetti, and Alejo Carpentier. These writers were chosen because each of them represents a different literary use of alienation. In addition they frequently modify traditional literary form in order to present specific aspects of the theme.

Because the focus of this study is on the appearance and development of alienation in the works of individual authors, a brief presentation of the history of the concept, followed by a short discussion of modern development and application of the idea, should suffice. The authors considered of most importance in terms of their contemporary studies of alienation are Erich Fromm (*The Sane Society* and *Man for Himself*) and Erich Kahler (*The Tower and the Abyss*). Of lesser importance are Fritz Pappenheim (*The Alienation of Modern Man*), R. D. Laing (*The Divided Self* and *The Politics of Experience*), and Wylie Sypher (*Loss of Self in Modern Literature and Art* and *Literature and Technology: The Alien Vision*).

Karl Marx formulated the basis for the modern concept of

alienation, although he was not the first nineteenth-century thinker to deal with it. Hegel in *The Phenomenology of the Mind* (1807) saw separation and estrangement at the center of every form of reality.[1]

Marx, however, was interested in the social application of the concept to his time and not in its validity as a universal principle. Most of the twentieth-century writers, with the exception of the existentialists, have been oriented toward the social application in their amplification of Marx's ideas.

Marx saw alienation arising from the relation of the worker to his product in an industrialized society: "This fact expresses merely that the object which labour produces—labour's product —confronts it as something alien, as a power independent of the producer. The product of labour is labour which has been congealed in an object, which has become material: it is the objectification of labour."[2] Because of this "the worker is related to the product of his labour as to an alien object" (p. 66). From this point of view Marx criticized nineteenth-century political economy because of its failure to consider the relation between worker and product.

Marx also examined the results of this relation, showing that, because modern industrial work is external to the essential being of the worker engaging in it, it is a form of self-denial, causing unhappiness and loss of self. The final result of this process of estrangement from both the product of labor and the act of labor, according to Marx, is that "man (the worker) no longer feels himself to be freely active in any but his animal functions ... and in his human functions he no longer feels himself to be anything but an animal" (p. 69).

Another aspect of the work relation is that "estranged labour estranges the species from man. It turns him from the life of the species into a means of individual man" (p. 71). Marx considered man as a species being and a conscious being, whose own life is an object for him. He felt that alienated labor made man's essential being not an object of life but, instead, a mere means to his existence. Thus he saw that the consequence of man being estranged from the product of his labor, from his life activity, and from his species being was the alienation of man from his fellow man and from the essential nature of mankind.

Marx later expanded these ideas and related them to his commodity theory, but the central idea of alienation arising from the relation between the worker and his labor or his product remained the same.

Erich Fromm's definition of alienation is the one most often quoted in the works consulted for this study. Herbert Read uses it as an introduction to *Art and Alienation*,[3] and it is the only definition used by Gerald Sykes in his two-volume anthology, *Alienation*.[4] Fromm states:

By alienation is meant a mode of experience in which the person experiences himself as an alien. He has become, one might say, estranged from himself. He does not experience himself as the center of his world, as the creator of his own acts—but his acts and their consequences have become his masters, whom he obeys, or whom he may even worship. The alienated person is out of touch with himself as he is out of touch with any other person. He, like the others, is experienced as things are experienced: with the senses and with common sense, but at the same time without being related to oneself and to the world outside productively.[5]

The value of this definition can be seen more clearly when it is compared to that of R. D. Laing, who says, speaking of twentieth-century man, "The condition of alienation, of being asleep, of being unconscious, of being out of one's mind, is the condition of the normal man."[6] This is an external description of symptoms that in no way shows the nature of the experience, as does Fromm's definition, and because of its vagueness it allows no further exploration of the state.

Fromm's designation of alienation as a mode of experience gives him full freedom to explore its social and economic origins, its present-day configuration, and the nature of alienated man in relation to himself and to mankind. In *The Sane Society* he chooses alienation as the central point in his analysis of contemporary social character because he believes it "touches upon the deepest level of modern personality" (p. 103).

Fromm, reflecting Marx's orientation, is specific about the framework of his investigation. He is interested in the effects of the mode of production and social and political organization on man. This interest leads him to a study of the elements specific to capitalistic production. In *The Sane Society*, to facilitate this study, he begins with a historical approach, briefly mentioning seventeenth- and eighteenth-century capitalism, and concentrating on its nineteenth- and twentieth-century forms.

For Fromm the twentieth century is marked by the disappearance of nineteenth-century personal exploitation, which is replaced by an anonymous exploitation that has the same end: the use of man by man. Other differences seen by him are changes from an exploitative hoarding orientation to a receptive marketing orientation, from competitiveness to teamwork, from increasing profit to steady income, from exploitation to spreading and sharing, from overt authority to anonymous authority, from individual conscience to conformity, and from a feeling of pride and mastery to a sense of powerlessness. These changes are, according to Fromm, the results of important social and economic differences between the centuries. They give rise, he believes, to the need for a certain kind of man, one who can cooperate in large groups, who has an increasing desire to consume, who has easily molded and standardized tastes, who feels free, and who nevertheless fits into society without friction.

Fromm views twentieth-century man, compared to man of the preceding centuries, as having undergone character changes, and, as already mentioned, the focus for his character analysis of contemporary man is alienation. This alienation, he believes, is mainly produced by one of the most important processes of capitalism: abstractification.

Two tendencies are seen by Fromm as being responsible for the growth of abstractification: the fact that all work in capitalist society is rewarded by money and not by goods or services, and the fact that the increasing division of labor results in more specialization of the function of the worker, with no relation of the worker to his product. His labor, divorced from any contact with the whole product, becomes machinelike. Management, which has contact with the whole product, sees it in terms of its exchange value and not as a concrete reality. Finally, Fromm says: "But in a society in which economic activities have become the main preoccupation of man, this process of quantification has transcended the realm of economic production, and spread to the attitude of man to things, to people, and to himself" (p. 105). Things are experienced as commodities, not as objects of vital attachment, and people are experienced in terms of their exchange value. The final result of abstractification is the dissolution of any concrete human frame of reference in modern life. *alienation*

Modern man, then, is seen by Fromm as totally alienated. The worker, separated from his product and with no vital interest in his work, is as alienated as the manager who deals with impersonal qualities and does not see his product as something useful.

Social forces, aside from business activity, are also described by Fromm as causing alienation. He considers the major factor here to be the anonymous character of our society, which is due to its size. Individual man feels no contact with or responsibility for the social system. This anonymity extends to his relation to his fellow man. Fromm describes the relationship as "one between two abstractions, two living machines, who use each other. The employer uses the ones whom he employs; the salesman uses his customers. Everybody is to everybody else a commodity . . ." (p. 126).

This anonymity also affects the relation of man to himself. Fromm believes that man experiences himself as an abstraction. The loss of dignity and the lack of experience of self have important effects. Fromm sees man, denied a primary experience of identity, developing a secondary sense of self in which he becomes a useful salable commodity, not a unique human being.

In the last part of his discussion of alienation in *The Sane Society*, Fromm describes various aspects of social character related to alienation. In his earlier book, *Man for Himself*, he had devel-

oped a system of character classification in which he fits the alienated man into the marketing orientation. In *The Sane Society* he
describes more concrete characteristics of alienated man. So-
cially he sees him as being submissive to anonymous authority, as
being conforming, and, because of his fear of being alone, as de-
siring acceptance. In addition, due partly to consumer orientation
and partly to the influence of Freud's ideas, contemporary man,
in Fromm's view, organizes his life around the principle of
nonfrustration.

Fromm also outlines other changes caused by the process he
has described that are of special interest with regard to alienation
and literature. Man has become more intelligent, he thinks, in
the sense of being able to work with concepts toward a practical
end, but he uses reason less in the sense of trying to understand
and to discover truth. The result is a loss of individuality and,
more importantly, the loss of a sense of reality, which Fromm sees
as another characteristic of the alienated personality. He states:
"... the fact is that modern man exhibits an amazing lack of realism for all that matters. For the meaning of life and death, for
happiness and suffering, for feeling and serious thought. He has
covered up the whole reality of human existence and replaced it
with his artificial, prettified picture of a pseudo-reality ..." (p.
153).

A reduced sense of reality raises the question of the mental
state of alienated man and of the position of alienation in terms of
sanity and insanity. Fromm's view is the following: "The person
who dreams while awake, that is, the person who is in touch only
with his inner world and who is incapable of perceiving the outer
world in its objective action context, is insane. The person who
can only experience the outer world photographically, but is out
of touch with his inner world, with himself, is the alienated person. Schizophrenia and alienation are complementary" (p. 183).

This view is, however, modified by another statement. Fromm
says:

... the neurotic person is an alienated person. His actions are not his own; while he is under the illusion of doing what he wants, he is driven by forces which are separated from his self, which work behind his back; he is a stranger to himself, just as his fellow man is a stranger to him. He experiences the other and himself not as what they really are, but distorted by the unconscious forces which operate in them. The insane person is the absolutely alienated person; he has completely lost himself as the center of his own experience; he has lost the sense of self. (P. 114)

insanity

These statements taken together indicate that alienation is a continuum based on degrees of loss of self. At one end are the insane, mainly schizophrenics, and at the other sane, but alienated, men, functioning in an alienated society. R. D. Laing seems to make this distinction, using the term *schizoid* for the sane but divided person, "the totality of whose [the schizoid's] experience is split in two main ways: in the first place there is a rent in his relation with his world and, in the second, there is a disruption of his relation with himself. Such a person is not able to experience himself 'together with' others or 'at home in' the world, but, on the contrary, he does not experience himself as a complete person but rather as 'split' in various ways, perhaps as a mind more or less tenuously linked to a body, as two or more selves, and so on."[7] He uses the term *schizophrenia* to describe the psychotic manifestation of the above tendencies. Wylie Sypher in *Loss of Self in Modern Literature and Art* uses the term *loss of self* to describe all degrees of alienation, from the socioeconomic defined by Marx to schizophrenia. Both Marx and Fromm also use this term as a synonym for alienation.

Bombal

A broad view of the subject seems advantageous in this study because of the complexities of the presentation of the alienated personality in literature. An approach limited to the socioeconomic aspects of alienation would ignore the internal emotional wealth of modern literature, especially when the emotions border on insanity. Schizophrenic art and imagery are important elements of modern art and cannot be ignored. Also, the use of a restricted socioeconomic definition would exclude existential alienation. The existentialists consider alienation to be an essen-

tial element of man's condition. As Camus describes it: ". . . in a
universe suddenly divested of illusions and lights, man feels an
alien, a stranger. His exile is without remedy since he is deprived
of the memory of a lost home or the hope of a promised land. This
divorce between man and his life, the actor and his setting, is
properly the feeling of absurdity."[8]

Alienation as leading to the existentialist experience is important in the next work to be discussed, *The Tower and the Abyss*
by Erich Kahler, which examines the condition of modern man
with a different perspective from that of Erich Fromm and Karl
Marx, even though Kahler discusses and includes some of their
ideas about alienation. Kahler is interested in the transformation
of man. He sees this process as "a state of transition from an individual form of existence to a supra-individual form of existence, the character of which is still in the dark."[9] His investigation
extends beyond the socioeconomic sphere into changes in man's
sensibility, transformation of reality, and an examination of the
existential experience as the culmination of the forces at work on
modern man. Alienation is seen to be an important element oper-
ating in a large sector of contemporary life.

Although the individual is the basic human unit, Kahler believes that he is modified by the group: "An individual, accord-
ingly, is not only an individual, he is at the same time more than
an individual inasmuch as he participates in groups" (p. 6). He
divides human groups into two classes, community and collective.
This is also the division used in *The Alienation of Modern Man*
by Pappenheim, who gives his source as *Gemeinschaft und
Gesellschaft* by Ferdinand Tönnies.[10]

Kahler's definition is as follows: "Groups, such as the family,
the tribe or the nation, which substantially as well as genealogi-
cally or historically precede their individual members and con-
stitute the basic, unconscious layers of the personalities of their
individuals, we call communities" (p. 7). Communities make and
transmit traditions and patterns of behavior. In addition their action on the individual is from within and on an unconscious level.

They act to form and enhance the individual, not to disrupt or destroy him.

He also defines collectives: "Political parties, work organizations, economic, occupational or technical combines, corporations, cooperatives, unions form a second type of group which we call collectives. These supra-individual or post-individual groups develop through the joining of pre-established individuals for some specific purpose. Collectives are established by common ends, communities derive from common origins" (p. 9).

The collective, of course, has become a characteristic of modern life. According to Kahler, it constructs standards and stereotypes that affect the individual externally, and it may cause disruption and splitting in the individual. Although these influences enter from without, consciously, they eventually reach the unconscious, where they can cause great change and damage. Kahler calls this the collective unconscious. "Here is stored up the residue of a host of mass stereotypes, slogans, conceptual simplifications, suggested or imposed attitudes, which by various means have sunk from consciousness into the unconscious" (pp. 10–11).

The origins of modern collectivism are found, in his opinion, in rationalism and technology, which have so shaped modern society that almost all processes tend to be collectivistic. Differing from Marx, he does not see economic or social concepts as being the cause of collectivization. "All these developments, the development of science, technology and industry, and their interpenetration, are but different aspects or ramifications of one evolutionary process; all of them lead eventually to collectivization and deindividualization. They split or invalidate the individual in various ways: apart from scientification, through specialization, functionalization, standardization, anonymization" (p. 22).

Although Kahler describes the social conditions causing alienation, he does not attempt a modern definition. It can be inferred that by alienation he means any loss of self or estrangement from nature or existence. He is clear, however, about the importance of this broad process. He states: "The history of man could very well be written as a history of the alienation of man" (p. 43).

Kahler does give a brief historical definition according to Hegel and Marx: "The concept of alienation recurring throughout this book in various forms requires a brief historical explanation. As originally used by Hegel and elaborated by Marx it meant a cleavage inherent in human nature: man being isolated and detached from universal nature is driven into opposition not only to all natural being, but implicitly to his own being: he parts with it through self reflection (i.e. through knowledge), and through labor" (p. 39).

Kahler sees the artist as being strongly affected by the modern conditions of alienation. As society becomes more collectivistic, the artist becomes more individualistic. Because of increasing isolation artist and audience become mutually exclusive. The language and techniques employed by artists are neither understood nor shared by the public. The new techniques have, however, created a new reality. Kahler states: "Thus the transformation going on in the arts is implicitly a transformation of what we call reality" (p. 152). Science—above all, physics—has been instrumental in the change. It has shown that the act of perception itself modifies the nature of the reality observed and that the observer's reality is always relative. Arts and letters, independently, Kahler believes, have made the same discovery.

Another aspect of science has greatly changed art. Psychoanalysis has provided artists with both new insight into the human personality, above all, by making the unconscious accessible, and new techniques, such as free association and stream of consciousness. This new insight produces new sensitivity in respect to the inner being. Kahler maintains that, "once we become attentive to the full contents of our continuous inner experience, a dimension is added which escapes all logical and chronological sequence" (p. 167). Thus time as an artistic continuum is destroyed.

The discovery of the personal unconscious was augmented by Jung's work with the collective unconscious. However, Kahler sees the deepest penetration into the inner being as that of the existentialist experience. He clearly separates it from existentialist philosophy, for which it serves as a nucleus. He believes it to be of great importance. "The existentialist experience may be seen as the accumulation, the concentration, indeed the quasi-physical climax of all the intellectual and moral crises of the past generations, and most especially of the crisis of the individual" (p. 169). The experience is characterized by decomposition of reason and abstraction, of terms and concepts, of objects, and of perception. "What ultimately remains, the only thing left, is existence itself, something inexpressible, indescribable. Some silly accident and incident without substance, in which the apparent beings find themselves caught involuntarily as it were, without being able to get rid of it, a supernumerary remainder of eternity, a saleté, a horror and disgust" (p. 176). The most complete literary description of this experience is seen in Sartre's novel *La Nausée*.

From the standpoint of alienation in literature this experience is of great interest. Because it is concerned with decomposition of objects and relationships, the images and structures used to describe the experience, or variations of it, may reflect the same decomposition. It may also be expected that personality will be fragmented if related to the experience. In the art of two of the Latin American authors to be studied here, Onetti and Bombal, personality fragment is of major importance.

Schizophrenic image and personality fragmentation show some of the same characteristics. Kahler does not relate his concept of the existentialist experience to schizophrenia. It has already been shown that schizophrenia may be considered as one of the boundaries of the territory covered by the concept of alienation. Thus image and personality fragmentation may be related not to the existentialist experience but to an extreme of alienation. The existentialist experience ends with a feeling of nothingness, of absurdity, of disgust. But this feeling is transmitted on a philosophical plane, and the experience is of philosophical importance in that it represents a coherent position in respect to existence. The fragmentation associated with schizophrenia is of a different order. Anton Ehrenzweig states: "True schizophrenic art only offers the surface experience of fragmentation and death without being redeemed by low-level coherence."[11] According to Ehrenzweig, the schizophrenic concentrates his energy on the fragmentation and does not allow his imagery to degenerate into emptiness and nothingness, because these fragments are all that remains to him of reality and he desperately wants to maintain this reality.

Thus it would seem that in order to determine the cause of fragmentation in art one has to ascertain whether it is part of a philosophical process leading to total dissolution of perception or whether fragmentation itself is the subject.

The foregoing discussion has covered the major features of alienation, briefly summarizing its history and presenting the ideas of modern commentators on the subject. Although its social and economic aspects have received their greatest attention, due mostly to the orientation Marx gave to the concept, other writers, such as Erich Kahler, have been more interested in the changes in human sensibility and in art resulting from the increasing importance of alienation in modern life.

Each of the authors chosen for this study seems to represent a different literary approach to alienation. María Luisa Bombal will be studied for her poetic modification of the theme. Juan Carlos Onetti is of interest because of his fragmented imagery resulting from exploration of the schizophrenic extreme of alienation. Alejo Carpentier, in whose work the socioeconomic elements of the theme are clearly visible, presents the cultural, artistic, and temporal aspects of the subject. In addition he puts alienation in contact with myth.

The emphasis will be on detailed study of individual and representative works. This method, with its reliance on internal evidence, should prove to be of more value than a generalized study of all the works of each author.

2. María Luisa Bombal: Alienation and the Poetic Image

María Luisa Bombal's first novel, *La última niebla*, was published in 1935 in Buenos Aires.[1] Her second novel, *La amortajada*, appeared in 1938. In 1947 she published *The House of Mist*, a novel in English based on *La última niebla*. These three books and a few short stories are all that she has written. In 1963 she was supposed to be working on another novel, *El Canciller*, which had originally been written in English in 1953 and was called *The Foreign Minister*.

María Luisa Bombal was chosen for this study because her treatment of alienation and loss of self seen in *La última niebla* represents two fundamental possibilities of the theme. She shows alienation, as a human experience, arising from personal, internal forces. Cedomil Goić states: "The world exposed in *La última niebla* has as its only base the personal existence of a woman reflectively turned upon her own destiny. This novel is distinguished by its personal structure."[2] This evaluation is not completely accurate. Although the personal element is predominant, there are social conditions, secondary in nature, that are important in terms of alienation. These will be examined later.

Bombal's literary treatment of the theme is its other fundamental possibility; the mode of presentation, development, and structure is poetic. Amado Alonso in his introduction to *La última niebla* emphasizes this: "The natural and direct form of narration is due, if I am not mistaken, to the sure knowledge of having a poetic concept to present . . . ."[3] Thus the nature and function of the imagery will be central to an examination of alienation and loss of self. It will be seen that concrete entities are used to symbolize and give poetic value to the alienated state. In addition, literary or thematic devices serve to distance the reader from the material, again creating a poetic experience of alienation.

Amado Alonso and Cedomil Goić both consider the date of publication of *La última niebla*, 1935, to be important because it marks a change in Chilean literature. Novelists up to then had been writing under the influence of naturalism, but around 1935 literature in Chile began to reflect surrealism and other contemporary movements of world literature. Goić says: "When María Luisa Bombal begins to write, she does so completely within the system of preferences of the new sensibility. She belongs to a younger generation than the surrealists; she moves with comfort and surety of means within the new rules imposed on the contemporary novel."[4]

Although the emotional states described in *La última niebla* are of great complexity and artfully constructed, the overall emotional trajectory of the protagonist is quite simple; starting from an unhappy marriage, the protagonist moves away from the real world into herself, through a process of increasing fantasy, and then is forced to retreat from this created world to face the realities of aging and emotional barrenness. Her interior movement is the focus of the novel.

However, there are exterior social dimensions that, although they never come into the foreground, provide a hidden influence that tends to push all Bombal's women into themselves, giving them a feeling, frequently not expressed, of lack of control over their lives. The position of women in the society described in her novels is the most outstanding of these forces, in that it makes marriage the central issue of their lives. On the emotional level, the most important one within Bombal's works, this position gives men the power of choice as opposed to women's relative help-lessness, turning men into an external alienating force. This is one of the meanings of the complaint in *La amortajada*: "Why, why is the nature of woman such that a man always has to be the center of her life?"[5]

Near the beginning of *La última niebla*, this social function of man—as the one with the power to choose and, consequently, to make woman feel a lack of control over her life—is emphasized. On their wedding night the husband asks:

"Why did we marry?"
"To marry," I answer.
Daniel gives a small laugh.
"Do you know that you've been lucky in marrying me?"
"Yes, I know," I reply, overcome with weariness.
"Would you have liked being a shriveled old maid, who sews for the
     poor of the hacienda?"
I shrug my shoulders.
"That's the fate awaiting your sisters . . ." (P. 42)

In direct opposition to the cultural background implied in this dialogue is the other important male-female relationship of the book, that between the woman narrator and her fantasized lover. It is characterized by a total lack of social or cultural context. The central element is that the narrator is desired as a woman, for herself and for her body. "Once nude, I remain seated on the edge of the bed. He moves away and contemplates me. Under his attentive glance I throw my head backwards, and this gesture fills me with intimate well-being. I hold my arms behind my neck, crossing and uncrossing my legs, and each movement brings me an intense and complete pleasure, as if, at last, my arms, my legs, and my neck had a reason for being. Even if this enjoyment were the only purpose of love, I would consider my-self well rewarded" (pp. 59–60).

Thus Bombal shows woman's position in society to be a force that causes alienation. This opinion is reinforced by another man-woman relation that is of less importance than the two already mentioned but causes the narrator's first emotional crisis. Her first encounter with passion in reality occurs when she surprises Regina and her lover embracing. This is a relationship that breaks all social rules, of course, and the aspect of scandal is stressed toward the end of the novel by the tragic results of the union. But the protagonist is driven to desperation by the realization that the love she desires exists outside social boundaries.

The achievement of extramarital love in Bombal's world involves the destruction of self, either physically, in the case of Regina, or mentally through escape into fantasy, in the case of the narrator in *La última niebla*.

Because of the existence of a social dimension, manipulated by the author through contrast and implication, Margaret Campbell's definition of a general theme in Bombal's works is somewhat inaccurate. She states, "In general the theme seems to consist of two parts: unrequited love and an attempt to deal with the situation."[6] However, Campbell's article does not examine or recognize that aforementioned social background. A better and broader statement of the theme would be that it is woman and love. This allows for the existence of the different types of love that are present in Bombal's works. If unrequited love were taken to be the main theme, it would be impossible to understand a story like "Islas nuevas," which is structured around the contrast between a sudden erotic passion and a shifting background of many kinds of love—the love of a man for his dead wife, of a mother for her son, and of father and son.

Another external aspect seen in *La última niebla* and most of the other works of Bombal is the contrast between town and country. It is probably most important in *La amortajada*, but it also plays a decisive role in *La última niebla*. This contrast is really one of a series of external elements used by the author to symbolize interior states, but in addition it has a structural function. Emotionally, the city represents lack of isolation and the presence of human contact (this is not true in *House of Mist*) and the country isolation and withdrawal. The protagonist

creates her lover in the city. Returning to the country, she begins
a long process of withdrawal and fantasy that leads to a state of
total alienation. The abrupt return to reality and the acceptance
of a barren life occurs in the city. Thus the major spatial movement of the novel involves elements that symbolize parallel emotional movement.

Amado Alonso considers the use of external elements to be a
characteristic of Bombal's art, giving it its special poetic quality.
"No descriptive note represents mere information or, even less, a
documentation of the objective; instead each one is an element
of interior life" (p. 20). He refers to the "structural role of the
accessory," saying: "The evident and admirable unity of tone in
this short novel arises because the author has used material according to poetic need and not according to literary convention:
as elements of architecture, not as themes of an exercise . . ." (pp.
15–16).

An example of the structural role of the accessory is seen at the
beginning of the novel when what at first glance seems to be an
insignificant detail is really that which provides access to the
most hidden parts of the narrator's character. When the narrator
surprises Regina and her lover, "two shadows suddenly separate,
one from another, with such little skill that the half undone hair
of Regina remains hanging from the buttons of the coat of a
stranger. Surprised, I look at them" (p. 46). She has, as already
mentioned, come face to face with the possibility of passion. But
the element that leads her to desperation is the hair caught between two lovers. Its immediate function is, of course, to symbolize the love between the two, but it starts a process of self-
examination that terminates with a full realization on the reader's
part of the narrator's mental and emotional condition.

The protagonist's first thought is a comparison between herself
and Regina: "I think of the too-tight braid that gracelessly
crowns my head" (p. 47). The hair symbolizes different emotional lives. Both Goić and Amado Alonso point out the parallel-
ism between Regina and the narrator. Alonso's description is
"Regina, a passionate life lived and real; she, a passionate life

dreamed and imagined" (p. 19). However, this parallel is still at the level of external character comparison. The next level of revelation in the novel, still based on the external element of hair, is a vision of the depths of the narrator's being. "In front of the mirror in my room, I undo my hair, also dark. There was a time when I wore it loose, almost touching my shoulders. Very straight, tightly drawn at my temples, it shined like glowing silk. My coiffure seemed to me, then, an unruly bonnet that, I'm sure, would have been pleasing to Regina's lover. Since then my husband has made me gather together my extravagant locks, because in everything I should force myself to imitate his first wife, his first wife, who, according to him, was a perfect woman" (p. 47).

She continues the comparison with Regina, showing how in the past they were equal, her hair as free as Regina's. The next step is the central reality of her emotional life. Her hair—and thus her life—is a form forced upon her by her husband to imitate his dead wife, an imitation she can never successfully carry out because the husband considers the first wife to have been perfect.

Bombal is telling the reader that the narrator has allowed herself to be destroyed, that she has allowed her body to become the imitation of another body, and that her function as a woman is not to be herself but to be another. The presentation of this state of total alienation from the self is arrived at through the use of a single external element—hair.

In the context of the book the hair incident, with all it reveals, is bracketed by two scenes that directly concern the body-self relation. The first is of great importance both structurally and emotionally. In it the major integrating element of the book, the mist, appears for the first time.

This first scene is the one in which the protagonist sees a child in its coffin. It is the first time she has seen a dead person. The physical contrast between a dead and a live body is emphasized; movement is opposed to imprisoned rigidity. After the initial external contrast, other reactions are successively more internal, as in the hair scene. First is a description of the dead girl's face as empty of all feeling. The visual impact of the body suggests a word—*silence*—to the narrator. "Silence, a great silence, a silence of years, of centuries, a dreadful silence that begins to grow in the room and in my head" (p. 44). The terror of the connotations of the word causes her to flee, but outside she finds more silence and a countryside covered with mist. The mist destroys physical reality. "I avoid silhouettes of trees so ecstatic, so vague, that I stretch out my hand to convince myself that they really exist" (p. 45).

She personifies the mist, and, because of its destruction of external reality, she feels that it is attacking her and her reality. "I exist, I exist—I shout—and I'm beautiful and happy! Yes. Happy! Happiness is nothing more than having a young, slim, and agile body" (p. 45).

Her reaction is unexpected and, at first glance, inexplicable. The terms she uses to affirm her existence are those of physical beauty and of happiness. The confusing part of her reaction is the further definition of happiness—having a young, slim, and agile body. It could be explained as the shallow idea of a young girl, but the emotions leading to it are not shallow. Only in the light of the following scene does this definition of happiness become more meaningful. By denying her own body, by allowing it to be turned into someone else's, the narrator has become alienated from herself, both physically and emotionally. Her frantic affirmation of existence is made in the face of a strong feeling of nonexistence. The linking of a body and happiness must be seen as an unfulfilled desire since she has in reality disassociated herself from her body. What she is really saying is that if she could feel vitally related to her body she would be happy.

R. D. Laing in *The Divided Self* describes this condition in the section on the unembodied self. He believes that the normal sense of being alive, of feeling real, is related to the way one feels one's body to be alive and real. However, many people become detached from their bodies through stress or illness. "The body is felt more as one object among other objects in the world than as the core of the individual's own being. Instead of being the core of his true self, the body is felt as the core of a false self, which a detached, disembodied, 'inner,' 'true' self looks on with tenderness, amusement, or hatred, as the case may be."[7]

The results of disembodiment, according to Laing, are that the unembodied self cannot participate directly in any aspect of life perceived through the body. The unembodied self becomes an onlooker and observes, controls, and criticizes the body's activities.

The scene following the narrator's encounter with Regina and her lover is important, because it specifically explores the body-self relation. Faced with Regina's intensity of life, and surrounded by two husbands and Regina's lover, the narrator cannot control her inner emotions. "It seems as though they had poured fire through my veins. I go into the garden, I flee" (p. 49). The reader does not know what these emotions are, nor does he have a very good idea of what caused the emotional outbreak. The narrator only describes Regina's "intensity of life, as though she were living an hour of interior violence" (p. 48). Her reaction is to seek solitude.

After the narrator flees, the reader becomes partially aware of her internal state through a series of physical images and their connotations, which convert to interior emotions. The first of these occurs when the narrator throws herself against a tree trunk. The physical sensations are not described, but their emotional impact is. "Oh, to throw my arms around an ardent body and tumble with it, entwined, suspended forever!" (p. 49). A tactile experience becomes a longing for the physical sensations of love. Once this desire for primary physical experience of love is expressed, the woman undresses to swim and explores her own body. "I didn't realize I was so white and so beautiful. The water lengthens my features, which assume unreal proportions. I never before dared to look at my breasts, now I look at them. Small and round, they seem to be diminutive flowers suspended above the water" (p. 49).

In one sense this is a moment of discovery. She wants love, but she wants to experience it through her own body, which she looks at for the first time and surrounds with physical sensations, both real and imaginary. However, something more complex is taking place, as the imagery of the scene reveals. Although the woman is searching for and encounters primary physical sensation, her vision connected with this experience is distorted. The imagery destroys the visual dimension of the physical world.

The description of her body in the water is an example of visual distortion; its outline lengthens to unreal proportions. Her breasts seem to detach themselves from her body to float on the water. To further destroy her form, the water plants entwine themselves about her body in a human caress.

Visual distortion is not limited to this scene. It is the dominant mode of vision in the book and is directly related to the central structural element of the work, the mist. The title of the novel indicates the importance that Bombal attached to the mist in relation to the entire work.

Amado Alonso discusses the function of mist, calling it a leitmotiv and saying, "But the constant poetic function of the mist is that of being the formal element in which the protagonist lives, engulfed" (p. 24). Cedomil Goić extends Alonso's concept: "Though one can conceive that the function of the mist is that of being the formal element of the dream, as does Amado Alonso, it really is much more than that and, as a point of narrative construction, definitely something else. We should not, in general, rely on the common conception of the dream atmosphere as something vague or nebulous. Dreams are sharp and clear. That which is shadowy is the border between dream and wakefulness."[8]

A detailed study of the use of mist in relation to its meaning in the crucial scenes of the novel will clarify its function as a literary element.

The first appearance of mist in the book has already been partially discussed. When the narrator flees from the child's funeral, she immerses herself in a mist-covered countryside. The exact wording of the description is important: ". . . a subtle mist has

diluted the countryside, and the silence is even more immense"
(p. 45). The mist distorts and destroys visual reality. It also becomes a barrier, isolating the protagonist from any emotional
contact with external reality. "I avoid silhouettes of trees so ecstatic, so vague, that I stretch out my hand to convince myself
that they really exist" (p. 45). The mist, personified, coincides
with her unexpressed internal emotional turmoil: "And because it
attacks me for the first time, I react violently against the assault
of the mist" (p. 45).

It has already been shown that at this point the narrator is
suffering a crisis of lack of identity, loss of self, and disembodiment. The mist in this scene is a complex symbol functioning on
several levels, providing further insight into her condition. It is a
visual quantitative measure of the narrator's isolation from external reality. It is also an emotional symbol of her internal confusion. Overall its function is to externalize her interior state of
withdrawal, confusion, and fantasy and, through its connotations, to create an emotional identification between reader and
character. It is important to realize that the narrator does not
describe her emotional state, leaving it to be deduced by the
reader from the use of an external symbol.

At the rational level there is an important opposition in this
scene that recurs through the novel: the existence of the protagonist against the nonexistence represented by the mist. Throughout the first part of the book, the mist invades more and more
territory and the protagonist is less and less in contact with herself. Before the crucial journey to the city, where she meets an
imaginary lover, the mist, functioning symbolically, has destroyed almost everything. "The mist closes in, more each day,
against the house. It has already made the pines disappear,
whose branches used to beat on the balustrade of the terrace.
Last night I dreamed that it was infiltrating, slowly, through the
crevices in the doors and windows, into my room, blurring the
color of the walls, the shape of the furniture, and entwining itself
in my hair, sticking to my body, it consumed everything, everything . . ." (p. 53). What remains is the image of Regina's face,

full of passion. Here mist is functioning as a clear symbol. The loss of body is central to the narrator's loss of self and complete alienation, and it is her body that the mist dissolves. The image of another body fulfilled by passion, that of Regina, withstands the assault of the mist. The mist is not the border between "dream and wakefulness." Instead it represents nonexistence destroying existence.

Also, in addition to its symbolic importance, the mist here has a structural function. By symbolically condensing the emotional condition of the protagonist to the point that only one element is able to resist the destruction of being, the book—and thus the narrator's life—must move in the direction of this element, toward a moment of passion.

Before this moment arrives, there is a brief section in which the narrator talks about her present and future life. She sees boredom and the lack of and impossibility of attaining love and desire. Facing her situation, she feels a desire for death. She says: "Of dying, yes, I feel capable. It is very possible to desire death because one loves life too much" (p. 56). For her, of course, the life she loves is not part of her existence; she hates the life she is leading.

This is the first time in the book that Bombal has described the situation of her central figure without using imagery as the method of description. This section seems to serve the function of firmly fixing the reader in a logical, rational relation to the situation of the protagonist so that this conviction of reality will carry over into the next scene, the encounter with a lover. Thus the reader and the protagonist are both convinced of the existence of the lover, and both coincide in their gradual discovery that he and the entire scene are fantasy.

In the love scene the imagery concerned with mist is reduced to its essential elements, with resonances, of course, of its earlier meaning. The physical setting is similar to others already seen; unable to sleep, suffering an emotional crisis, the narrator goes out at night, into the fog-covered city. The imagery refers to the scene in which she fled from the funeral and leaned against a

tree, converting the physical sensation of the tree into a desire
for physical love. Bombal, using the same images, relies upon the
memory of emotions already created to set the scene. "Through
the darkness and the mist I glimpse a small plaza. As if in the
country I lean, exhausted, against a tree. My cheek searches for
the humidity of its bark" (p. 56). What follows is a complete
love scene that later is seen to be fantasy.

Mist as an image occurs only once during the scene, and the
narrator makes a clear and concise statement about its meaning.
This occurs when her lover takes her to his bedroom. "All the
warmth of the house seems to have been concentrated here. The
night and the mist can beat in vain against the windowpanes;
they will not succeed in introducing a single atom of death into
this room" (p. 58). She is, of course, referring not to physical
death but, instead, to death in life, to nonexistence caused by
lack of a body to experience love.

Because the love scene is put forth as the negation of the world
symbolized by the mist, the form that love takes is of great importance to an understanding of the narrator's loss of self and the
conditions that seem to allow her to temporarily (and mis-
takenly) experience herself. A careful study of the scene reveals
its basic unreality.

The first unreal aspect is that no verbal communication takes
place. The communication is at an emotional level and corresponds to the wishes of the narrator. The physical contact is described in terms of her gratification alone.

More important is the way the narrator refers to her body as a
separate entity, expressing her feeling of disembodiment. "The
beauty of my body yearns for, at last, its share of homage" (p.
59). Not only is she maintaining detachment from her body, as
shown by her point of view, but she is also removed from her
feelings. "I embrace him and with all my senses listen" (p. 60).
The use of the present tense in the description adds to the feeling
of detached observation.

The narrator's disembodiment and detachment are reinforced
a few pages later when, becoming aware of the passing of time

and of advancing age, she looks back upon her moment of love and says, "What difference does it make that my body withers, if it knew love!" (p. 64). This quotation shows how she remains separate even from the memory of the central event in her life, thinking of it as something that happened to her body and not to her intimate self.

At any rate, it is clear that the forces of disembodiment and loss of self that caused her desperation are present to a great degree in what she sees as a moment of fulfillment. This fact alone casts the reality of the scene in doubt, even without the other unrealistic details concerning the lover and the form of the encounter. The rest of the book is concerned with the gradual discovery by the protagonist of the fantasy of the situation.

As far as the relation of mist as an image to the scene is concerned, one more aspect should be mentioned. When the narrator leaves her lover, she describes the trees, again, as immobile, but the mist is not described. Its absence is important in that it underlines the mist's function as a symbol referring to the interior state of the protagonist. It and its threat of nonexistence are absent after a moment of ostensible fulfillment.

The experience, of course, changes the existence of the narrator, and the images connected with her interior life have to reflect this change. However, several problems arise from the direction and form her life takes after what she has described as an experience of love.

The general emotional movement of the rest of the novel is easy to delineate. The narrator moves farther into her fantasy world. At the same time she feels a growing need for definite proof of her lover's existence, a need that leads to the eventual destruction of the myth she had created. During this process the mist plays an important role in several crucial scenes.

The first problem in dealing with the narrator's emotional life concerns her extreme passivity after her moment of love. She makes no effort to contact her lover or to have any further experience. She says: "My love for 'him' is so great that it overcomes the pain of his absence. It is sufficient for me to know that he

exists, that he feels and remembers in some corner of the world"
(p. 66). There is no imagery to aid in the interpretation of this
emotional state. The only help is the narrator's own words in the
following paragraph: "My only desire is to be alone to dream
freely. I always have so much to think about! Yesterday afternoon, for example, I left suspended a scene of jealousy between
my lover and myself" (p. 66).

Her words reveal that her experience of love did not help her
to establish contact with herself but, instead, allowed her to
create a false self, building a world around this self. The only
way to explain her passivity is to consider that the object of her
desire is her fantasy world rather than real experience, which is
forbidden her by the form of her external existence. Her response
to her initial loss of self is to create a myth that allows her to increase her alienation by erecting a fantasy, false self. Sustaining
this false self makes conflict with reality inevitable.

Bombal again employs mist as an image when the narrator
seeks affirmation of the existence of her lover. She first looks for
concrete evidence and finds it in her straw hat, which she believes she lost when she met her lover. This evidence is not emotionally satisfying, but her lover's appearance is.

The setting for the scene is interesting in itself. The narrator is
bathing in the pond. The importance of the pond in revealing
her state of separation from her body has already been shown.
Thus her physical actions, on a symbolic plane, show continuing
separation from her body. When the lover comes, he comes
through the mist. "I was emerging from those luminous depths
when I saw in the distance, through the mist, completely closed,
a coach coming silently, as though it were an apparition" (p. 70).
Her lover is in the coach. He stops, looks at her nude body, and
goes on "as if the mist had devoured him" (p. 71). These two
quotations couple mist with unreality and nonexistence. In the
first the lover is in the mist and appears unreal. In the second the
mist destroys even his ephemeral existence by seeming to swal-
low him. Thus the mist in this scene seems to be an external
symbol related to the existence of the lover, and only by extra-

polation does it relate to the interior condition of the narrator. The image that does serve as an indicator of her emotional state is the pond, referring to associations previously established in the first part of the book.

In addition, the importance of the narrator's body-self relation is emphasized in that when her lover does look at her, he looks at her nude body, reminding the reader of the love scene and the importance the protagonist attached to having her body admired.

The unreality of the lover is more pronounced in this scene, and there is an additional feature that provides a new dimension. The narrator cannot communicate with or contact her lover for the simplest of reasons: she does not know his name. This inability could be construed as an indicator of how far her loss of self and fragmentation have progressed. She is unable to communicate with a fantasy of her own creation.

Her immediate need for verification of her lover's existence is another indication of increasing difficulty, which she counters with attempts to believe that he is near. She also renews physical contact with her husband. She cannot accept the physical gratification resulting from this contact, because she feels guilt about betraying her lover. However, the physical pleasure allows her to realize more clearly his importance. "My lover is for me more than a love; he is my reason for being, my yesterday, my today, my tomorrow" (p. 88). This is a clear statement of her desire to maintain a fantasy world and a fantasy self in preference to a real world and an authentic self, and in retrospect it helps to explain her passivity in the real world.

Mist imagery is again a central element in the crucial scene in which reality finally overpowers her fantasy world. Two events that are the direct cause of the scene need to be examined beforehand because of their aid to understanding.

The first event is the renewed communication with her husband, which exposes her to direct physical gratification and, however unacceptable, renews her contact with her own body. Also, her husband is responsible for pushing her into direct action to verify the existence of the lover; he denies that she ever went out in the night and thus destroys the factual basis of her adventure.

The other critical event is Regina's attempted suicide. In terms of plot it allows the narrator to return to the place of her encounter. It also provides part of the closed structure of the book. The narrator's emotional trajectory starts when she is confronted by Regina and her lover and ends when she is faced with the results of Regina's affair.

The major function of the scene is to provide the narrator with an objective way of examining and evaluating her own life by comparing it with Regina's. "Behind Regina's gesture is an intense feeling, an entire life of passion. Only a memory maintains my life, a memory I keep alive day by day so that it doesn't disappear. A memory so vague and so distant that it seems to me almost a fiction" (p. 92). The perspective gained makes her realize the extent of her misfortune and unhappiness, something she has never done before. This is the first encounter she has had with her real self, that is, the self based in reality, and the result is a decision to abandon her passivity, to search for her lover or to prove his existence.

The mist has a minor role in the aforementioned scene as background to the emotional discovery that is the major element. When the protagonist comes into Regina's hospital room, she sees Regina in bed, turns away, and presses her head "against the windowpane blurred with fog" (p. 92). The physical situation is reminiscent of the love scene; the mist is outside and cannot enter the room. Whereas in the love scene it was ostensibly the life created by the intensity of passion that restrained the mist and its symbolic meaning of nonexistence, in the hospital the encounter is with truth. The only thing that can be said then, based on the elements presented within the scene, is that the opposition is between a moment of truth through self-discovery and the surrounding mist-covered world where truth is absent. Obviously, at this point the symbolic meaning of the mist is the total of all the meanings attached to it during the course of the novel.

The first few lines of the next crucial scene support this interpretation. The protagonist again goes out in the city at night in an active search for her lover and for the place where her encounter occurred. It must be emphasized that this is the first time she has actively tried to establish contact. She describes the night: "In the middle of the mist, which immaterializes everything" (p. 93). This immaterialization has been the basic symbolic function of the mist throughout the novel; it destroys reality. In this part of the scene it prohibits her from determining the physical reality of the surroundings in her search.

An additional and highly important quality of the mist is described. "The mist, with its smoky barrier, prohibits any direct vision of beings and of things, provoking a withdrawal into one's self" (p. 94). That the mist frequently is a symbolic poetic externalization of the narrator's interior emotional state has already been inferred from the previous scenes, but this clear statement by the protagonist indicates a much greater degree of self-knowledge and allows the reader to understand logically what before had to be inferred symbolically.

In addition, the narrator's definition of the action of the mist upon herself gives the entire scene symbolic meaning. She is wandering in the mist of her fantasy, within herself. The mist in this scene thus has become a symbol of the emotional vision of the protagonist, a vision about to be shattered against reality.

The protagonist finds a house she believes to be her lover's. But it is not; it is furnished in bad taste, and its master, blind, had died fifteen years before. Her dream of love can no longer stand.

When she realizes that all has been a fantasy, she talks about the destructive power of the mist in the same words she had used to describe its action upon her lover when he appeared while she was bathing in the pond. Also, her words show that she has abandoned her struggle to maintain the fantasy and instead has accepted the reality of her unhappiness. "Besides, why struggle? It was my destiny. The house, and my love, and my adventure, all have disappeared in the mist" (p. 98).

The mist as described here by the protagonist is an external

destructive force. It is capable of destroying emotions and fantasies in addition to physical reality. However, behind the protagonist's description of the external function of the mist, there
is another level of meaning. The narrator's words must be examined in the light of the perspective possessed by the reader
with his knowledge of the emotional life of the protagonist and
of the change that has just taken place in that life. At various
places in the novel the mist, at its maximum level of emotional
intensity, has been a symbol of the protagonist's emotional vision,
physically representing her peculiar inability to distinguish between reality and fantasy. When she finally and unequivocally
can identify reality and can establish contact with herself, she
describes her fantasies as being destroyed by the same element
that has previously destroyed reality. The tone of her statement
puts the final action of the mist in the past, but at the same time
it generalizes its action. Thus the mist acquires a universal quality as a mysterious force inimical to human happiness. At the
same time it maintains its individual character as a form peculiar
to a large part of the protagonist's life. The former meaning is
well described by Cedomil Goić: "The specific function of the
mist is to represent the ominous, the presence of the hostile forces
of the world."[9]

In part, the final scenes represent the triumph of this hostile
force. Although the protagonist has abandoned a false self she
constructed through fantasy, the real self she encounters is that
of a desperately unhappy woman, aging, with no possibility of
future happiness. She further realizes, again through Regina's
life, that it is not love she is lacking. What she has missed is direct, primary experience, be it love or pain, and by her own
nature she has denied herself such experience. "And I feel, suddenly, that I hate Regina, that I envy her suffering, her tragic
adventure, and even her possible death. I'm assailed by a furious
desire to shake her violently, asking her what she has to complain
about, she, who has had everything! Love, vertigo, and abandon"
(p. 100). The protagonist's realization that she has wasted her
own life leads her to attempt suicide. Her tragedy, the triumph

of the hostile forces, is that the self and the life she accepts are without life and without hope. "But an implacable destiny has robbed me even of the right to search for death, it has been binding me, slowly, insensibly, to old age without fervor, without memories . . . without past" (p. 102).

The mist is the closing image. The narrator, after being stopped by her husband from throwing herself in front of a car, accepts the fact that what remains of her life is linked to his. "I follow him to carry out an infinity of insignificant tasks; to fulfill an infinity of pleasant frivolities; to cry by habit and to smile because of duty. I follow him to live properly, to die properly, some day.

"Around us the mist gives things a character of definitive immobility" (p. 102).

This acceptance is of course a complete change. The narrator is no longer totally alienated from her everyday life, and she has abandoned her false fantasy self. To a lesser degree than before, her being remains split between unfulfilled desires and the knowledge that in the life she has accepted these longings can never be gratified. The rest of her life will be lived in the unhappiness caused by this split.

In the final sentence the mist symbolically defines this frozen state of unhappiness. "Around us the mist gives things a character of definitive immobility." The universal meaning of the mist, dominant in the final scenes, is functioning here. It is a generalization and judgment applied to the rest of the narrator's life.

Although there is no direct textual evidence, other than the ambiguous parallel between the word *final* in the title (*última*) and the phrase "definitive immobility," it seems obvious that the meaning shown by the mist in the last sentence of the book is that referred to by the title.

This detailed study of the mist as it appears in different scenes has shown that it is an element used by Bombal for a variety of purposes and with many different meanings. It is used to describe both interior and exterior conditions with respect to the protagonist, and it ranges in meaning from a simple symbol of non-existence to a universal symbol of forces opposed to human happiness. The total and final effect of the use of a multifaceted element is the sense of mystery produced as the different meanings merge into a vague, diffuse, complex reaction to the element with each new appearance. The scene-by-scene analysis has stressed the separate meanings deduced from the context of the situation, but the response to the accumulation of meanings should not be ignored.

The same sense of mystery surrounds the character of the protagonist. Although it is possible to analyze the basis of her actions, no information is given about the conditions that caused them. Thus the reader sees the loss of self beginning with the acceptance, emotional and physical, of her role as replacement for her husband's first wife; yet her reasons for accepting this role are not presented. Again, although her passivity after her imagined encounter with a lover can be explained, her final passivity in the face of an immobile, unhappy life has no explanation within the novel. Thus the protagonist's character and the major literary element used throughout the book—the mist—coincide in that their meaning and nature are limited to the events presented in the book and do not extend beyond the actual narrative content.

However, one aspect of the image of the mist that is totally outside the book should be discussed: the quality and meaning of the type of vision associated with the image. Mist as a physical phenomenon has several visual characteristics. It destroys a sense of depth. Without a sense of depth, visual impressions become superficial. This superficiality is characteristic of schizoid vision. Joseph Gabel, in his work on alienation, describes several aspects of this type of vision: "Finally, the live space of melancholics is characterized by the loss of the dimension of living depth, and this, in apparently paradoxical fashion, is followed by the exaggeration of live distances, which change from human to super-human."[10] Anton Ehrenzweig defines a similar kind of vision: "Depersonalized vision tends to have a clearer peripheral field, but is also flatter, and in a sense unreal."[11] He further describes schizoid vision in art: "True schizophrenic art only offers the surface experience of fragmentation and death without being redeemed by low-level coherence" (p. 122).

The schizoid disembodiment of the protagonist has already been described, but her other schizoid traits have not. Her retreat into a world of fantasy corresponds to a description by R. D. Laing: "The unrealness of perception and the falsity of the purposes of the false-self system extend to feelings of deadness of the shared world as a whole, to the body, in fact, to all that is, and infiltrate even to the 'true' self. Everything becomes entirely unreal or 'phantasticized,' split, and dead, and no longer able to sustain what precarious sense of its own identity it started with."[12] This correspondence should not be surprising because the difference between alienation and schizophrenia is one of degree and not of kind. Erich Fromm considers the two conditions to be complementary and Erich Kahler treats them as different stages of the same process. R. D. Laing, seeming to utilize the same concepts as Kahler, makes the further distinction, followed here, between schizoid and schizophrenic: "The term schizoid refers to an individual the totality of whose experience is split in two main ways: in the first place, there is a rent in his relation with his world and, in the second, there is a disruption of his relation with himself."[13] The schizoid, however, is sane, whereas the schizophrenic is psychotic.

Nevertheless, the exact psychological classification and analysis of the protagonist in *La última niebla* are not important. Her character has been presented through implication, suggestion, and connotation, not through analysis. What is important is the additional use of mist to evoke a poetic qualitative and quantitative experience of an abnormal state of mind. This is the highest poetic level of the novel in that the reader emotionally and irrationally shares the protagonist's experience of life.

3. Juan Carlos Onetti: Alienation and the Fragmented Image

Juan Carlos Onetti has been a prolific author and an important one.[1] His first publication, *El pozo,* in December of 1939, marked a new stage in Uruguayan literature. Angel Rama describes the cultural background of Onetti and *El pozo*: "From 1938 to 1940 a fracture occurs in Uruguayan culture that opens, through the course of a new interpretation of ethical and artistic values, a creative period that, after intense struggle, will control the intellectual life of the country. This fracture coincides with the rise of a generation of writers who vary between twenty and thirty years of age, who in part provoke it, and whose action is projected on the particularly disordered background of national and international life of those years."[2]

El pozo was immediately followed by a larger novel, *Tierra de nadie,* in 1941. Another novel, *Para esta noche,* appeared in 1943. After this Onetti did not publish a major work until 1950, when *La vida breve* appeared. This is considered by many critics to be his best and most ambitious work. *La vida breve* was followed by two novels: *Los adioses* (1954) and *Para una tumba sin nombre* (1959). A somewhat longer novel, *El astillero,* was published in 1961. His last published novel to date is *Juntacadáveres,* which appeared in 1965.[3]

In addition to writing novels, Onetti has been a productive short-story writer. *Un sueño realizado y otros cuentos* was published in 1951. Another collection, *El infierno tan temido y otros cuentos*, came out in 1962. All of these are in *Cuentos completos*, published in 1967.[4] Mario Benedetti has described the nature of Onetti's stories compared to his novels: "Onetti's stories show, as soon as they are compared to his novels, two notable differences: the obligatory restriction of material, which simplifies its dramatism, affirming it, and also the relative abandonment—the unconscious transfer—of the subjective burden that is borne by the protagonist in the novels and that generally is a limitation, at times a monotonous insistence of the narrator."[5]

Many of his works, however, fall into the territory between novel and short story. The relative complexity of theme and the quantity of subjective elements associated with it, as mentioned by Benedetti, seem to be reasonable criteria to separate short novels from short stories. Thus *El pozo*, although of few pages, is in Onetti's novelistic mode because of the presence of many themes and because of the subjective, ambiguous presentation of these themes. "El infierno tan temido" is structured around one action and its consequences and is very limited thematically. "Jacob y el otro" is of greater length than the other stories, but is again characterized by simplicity. A future action, a wrestling match, is the cause of all of the story's movement, and there are few complications of imagery or subjective content.

Complexity and ambiguity are the major characteristics of Onetti's novels. Emir Rodríguez Monegal, comparing him with his contemporaries, describes the difficulties and rewards of reading Onetti: "Anyone will notice the suspicious monotony of his figures, the unilaterality of descriptive method, the symbolism (at times excessive) of his actions and characters, the deliberately baroque development that obstructs the reading, the isolated traces of bad taste. But none of those in his category (urban and realist) attains the violence and lucidity of his declarations, the sure quality of his art, which overcomes superficial realism and moves with passion among symbols."[6]

Augmenting this complexity is, as Harss and Dohmann point out, Onetti's way of dealing with content. "He is less interested in arriving at the truth of a situation than in isolating its components—its alternatives—which are likely to yield as many falsehoods as facts."[7] As will be seen in the discussion of *El pozo*, the reader must separate falsehoods from facts in order to understand the character of the protagonist and the nature of the problems facing him.

At the stylistic level much of Onetti's complexity is not original. It stems from the acknowledged influence of other writers, particularly Faulkner.[8] Dos Passos has been important in influencing the structure of Onetti's earlier work, above all *Tierra de nadie*. The other major foreign influence has been Celine. Roberto Arlt, according to Harss and Dohmann, is also of importance.[9]

Onetti's creation of a fictional geography would seem to be obviously due to Faulkner, but the major differences between Yoknapatawpha County and Santa María are indicative of the different goals of the authors. Faulkner gives his creation all the appearance of reality. More importantly, his use of location is centrifugal. He peoples his county with generations of families and explores its history from the beginning. His characters stand apart from one another and are united by their roots in the land and its history. Readers of Onetti know that Santa María is a creation, because they were present at its birth in *La vida breve*, where it is an invention of the main character, Brausen. The major difference is, however, that Onetti's world is centripetal. The external features serve only as a frame for internal chaos. All the characters fall toward this center point, and individuals do not stand out as they do in Faulkner. Onetti himself, in *Juntacadáveres*, has best described his typical character in Santa María: "He isn't a person; he is, like all the inhabitants of this strip of the river, a determined intensity of life molding itself in the form of his own mania, his own idiocy."[10]

Alienation is a major feature of Onetti's internalized world. Mario Benedetti recognizes this when he states that "the dramatism of his fiction is derived precisely from a reiterated verification of alienation, from the forced incommunication endured by the protagonist and, therefore, by the author."[11] Harss and Dohmann, writing of the main figure in *El pozo*, generalize on the importance of alienation in Onetti. "Even in his alienation, or because of it, he is representative of a time and place, a frame of mind, an epoch. It is this fact that gives his experiences relevance and validity. To have realized this is Onetti's merit."[12]

Harss and Dohmann have also pointed out another aspect of alienation in Onetti. "What this amounts to in practice is that reading an Onetti book is a schizophrenic experience. The reader is in constant flux between the mind or perceptions of the narrator-protagonist and those of the author, the two being practically indistinguishable."[13] They do not explore this aspect any further. In the discussion that follows, an attempt will be made to show how Onetti's artistic manipulation of the schizophrenic experience (or the experience of extreme alienation) produces a unique imagery and an unusual sensation for the reader of participation in an alienated world.

Due to the cohesiveness of Onetti's fictional world in terms of characters and content, with the exceptions of *Tierra de nadie* and *Para esta noche*, and also to the presence of recurring reworked themes, with the same people in different situations and stages of development, the procedure followed in this study will be to examine carefully a limited number of works, while attempting to show their relation to others, in terms of theme and technique. *El pozo*, because of its relative clarity and simplicity of themes, compared to their later ambiguity, and because of the importance critics have attached to it, will be studied first.

The protagonist of *El pozo*, Eladio Linacero, is one of the best examples in contemporary South American literature of the completely alienated man. Angel Rama considers the main theme of the novel to be "radical solitude." He divides this solitude into two aspects, physical and emotional. The protagonist is physically isolated, alone in a room, and he is emotionally isolated, having cut all ties with other human beings, according to Rama.[14]

The story is, however, built not around the solitude of the protagonist but, rather, around his attempts at communication. The time elapsed, less than one day, is limited to how long it takes Linacero to write his first-person narrative. The author-protagonist gives the reader fragments of past and present personal history and an ostensibly complete picture of his emotional life.

Based on the nature of the attempts at communication, the novel divides itself into two parts. The first is concerned with the narrator's presentation of his present situation, the beginning of the act of writing, a statement of purpose that, as will be seen, is both aesthetic and emotional, and, finally, the first attempt at written communication, directed toward the reader. The second part is primarily a description of past frustrated attempts at communication with other people. In each case the hidden content of these efforts reveals more of the narrator's condition than he is aware of presenting. The result of the narrative is that Eladio Linacero reaches a crisis of self-hate, induced by a confrontation with his own existence. The novel ends at the moment of his maximum desperation.

It is evident from the foregoing synopsis that literary creation is an important theme in *El pozo*, and this fact has been noted by most of the critics who have studied the work. What is less evident is that the theme is shaped by and develops within the restrictions imposed upon it by the personality of the protagonist. Because extreme alienation is the outstanding characteristic of the narrator, *El pozo* provides a unique opportunity to examine the relations between alienation and literary creation.

The first paragraph of the novel indirectly introduces the theme of creation, in an unexpected context. "A while ago I was walking around the room and it suddenly occurred to me that I was seeing it for the first time. There are two cots, broken-down chairs without seats, sun-faded papers, months old, fixed in the window in place of glass."[15] The room is important as the boundary of the narrator's physical solitude and as the setting for the entire story. It is also the only place left to the narrator in his retreat from the world. At the beginning of the narration, the room has been a fixture and a delimitation of his life for some time, to the point that he is no longer aware of its existence. Yet, upon starting an attempt at communication, he sees it again, with new perspective. The inference is that he is entering into a new relation with his surroundings, no matter how reduced they are, caused by the act of creation. This interpretation is supported by the first statement he makes about the act of writing, a page later. "I found a pencil and a pile of pamphlets under Lázaro's bed, and now nothing bothers me, neither the filth, nor the heat, nor the wretches in the patio. It is certain that I don't know how to write, but I'm writing about myself" (p. 8).

The quoted lines also illuminate a feature of the first paragraph of the story that will have meaning later and will be seen in other works by Onetti. The word *filth* describes the emotional impact of Linacero's environment, especially that of the room. Yet, in the already quoted first paragraph, when he is looking at the room as though it were for the first time, he does not generalize on what he sees. Instead he describes isolated parts, substituting them for a totality of vision.

This form of vision emerges more clearly in his first description of a person, a prostitute. "She was a small woman, with pointed fingers . . . I can't remember her face; I see only her shoulder chapped by the whiskers that had been rubbing it, always that shoulder, never the right one, the skin reddened and the fine-fingered hand pointing it out" (pp. 7–8). Two fragments—fingers and a shoulder—serve to represent a human being. The narrator remembers nothing else about her.

The function and meaning of this type of vision do not become evident immediately. It is only through the additional information given by the narrator and through contrast with another kind of vision present in his dreams that the reader can begin to define their importance.

Before Linacero breaks the time sequence of the first section to describe a past event and the dream constructed around it, he talks about himself and his intentions with respect to what he is going to write. His self-description both directly and indirectly defines his alienation.

His reaction to a child playing in the mud and to the activities of people seen from his window shows several alienated attitudes. He says, "I realized that there really were people capable of feeling tenderness for that" (p. 8). The scene that provoked the response was banal but not repulsive. An underlying disgust for life is the obvious bias that explains the incongruity of the response. Linacero's lack of toleration of other viewpoints implies confidence in the correctness of his reaction. The possibility that he has been disillusioned by the failure of humanistic ideals is fairly well negated by the absence of repulsive elements in the scene. However, his disillusionment is implied by a value judgment in another description of people, "the wretches in the patio" (p. 8). At this point in the work, there is not enough evidence to assess the narrator's idealism, although the possibility of projection of his unhappiness and disgust to other people suggests itself. As the novel progresses, idealism is seen to be a veneer covering Linacero's radical irrational disgust with life.

Further motives for Linacero's efforts toward written communication are given. The next day will be his fortieth birthday. "I never would have imagined forty this way, alone and surrounded by filth, enclosed in a room. But this doesn't make me melancholic. Nothing more than a feeling of curiosity about life and a bit of admiration for its ability to always disconcert. I don't even have any tobacco" (p. 8). He obviously considers the birthday to be of importance as a personal dividing line and as a way of measuring his solitude. He implies disillusionment due to unfulfilled expectations, but he does not attach much importance to it. The description stresses his physical solitude and, at the same time, seems to show philosophical acceptance of his emotional alienation from life and his distrust of it. To claim curiosity would seem to mean that his removal of himself from life has not caused too much difficulty.

The last sentence—"I don't even have any tobacco"—is apparently a *non sequitur*, yet the negative relates it to the rest of the paragraph. Only in retrospect does its meaning become clear. At the end of *El pozo*, when Linacero has reached a state of total desperation, he gives another definition of himself. "I'm a solitary man who smokes anyplace in the city" (p. 36). The habit of smoking has become his only human action in the face of total alienation, withdrawal, desperation, and disgust. Thus, in the first part of the work, when he says he does not have any tobacco, it would seem that he is making a symbolic statement about the depth of his solitude that belies his more rational statement of philosophical fortitude. Other examples of the same technique of symbolic commentary that support this interpretation will be seen later.

Onetti often uses two levels of repeated actions: habitual actions and repeated meaningless actions. They have as a common ground repetition, but habitual actions are meaningful in that they reflect and define the existence of the person involved. Repeated meaningless actions are external to the character of the person but may have meaning in relation to the book. An example of habitual action is seen in *Los adioses*; the protagonist is most frequently seen in the act of drinking, and this act is his major connection with the narrator.

In addition to the function of these two types of action with respect to the description of characters, they also are major structural elements. In *Para una tumba sin nombre* the action of smoking a pipe is used to separate the narrative sections and to represent the narrator's periods of communication. It has a similar function in *La cara de la desgracia*. Habitual action is raised to the level of ritual in *Tan triste como ella*, where it is central to the understanding of the protagonist's suicide. When she can no longer struggle against the vegetation in her garden, life ceases to have meaning for her. In *El astillero* repeated meaningless action, reading former business transactions, becomes a defensive ploy in Larsen's fight to endure.

One of the significant differences between Onetti's novels and his short stories is the relative lack of repeated action patterns of both types in the latter. "El infierno tan temido" initially seems to be built around repetition, the sending of pornographic photographs, but the action is really cumulative rather than repetitive:

it is the vengeance taken by the wife for damage done by her husband. The stories probably lack these patterns because they are concerned with one action and its immediate consequences, whereas the other works emphasize an expanding series of possibilities, conflicts, and ambiguities arising from any situation or action.

The aesthetic result of this technique is a fragmentation of the character or characters involved. The repetition destroys what would be a normal process of development and response, so that, instead of gaining recognition and familiarity with the literary figure through cumulative exposure, the reader is constantly thrown back to the uncertainty and ambiguity of his first contacts with the character. Onetti's frequent use of a narrator separated from the protagonist would also seem to indicate his intention to distance the reader from his characters. In effect this is planned alienation of the reader from the content of the work.

El pozo is atypical of Onetti's works in that the first-person narration has an immediacy and a directness not seen in most of the others. There are probably two reasons for this. First, it is an early work and Onetti had not yet developed the use of ambiguity and multiplicity of planes that characterize his later writing. *Tierra de nadie* and *Para esta noche* show a developing ability in the manipulation of these factors. *La vida breve* represents their full development. The second reason is the importance of the theme of communication in *El pozo*. The aforementioned tendencies and techniques would blunt the impact and restrict the development of this theme. *Para una tumba sin nombre* shows the application of these techniques to the theme of communication, with resultant complete ambiguity as to motives and content.

Communication is uppermost in Linacero's mind when he reaches what he calls "the point of departure" in his attempt to write. "But now I want to do something different. Something better than the story of the things that happened to me. I would like to write the story of a soul, of it alone, without the events in which it had to participate, wanting to or not. Or of dreams.

From some nightmare, the most distant that I remember, to the adventures in the log cabin" (p. 9).

That these two artistic possibilities are of equal value to the narrator is obvious, but at first there does not seem to be any explanation as to why they should be equal. The first, "the story of a soul," free from the events in which it had to participate, is an undefinable and unobtainable goal, an artistic ideal. The other, the story of dreams, is, as the reader knows retrospectively, the essence of the emotional life of the narrator. Thus the second possibility is really a particularization or individualization of the first. That the narrator does not make the logical link is not important. In fact, he goes to the opposite extreme and tries to deny the role dreams play in his life. "What is curious is that, should anyone say of me that I'm a dreamer, it would annoy me. It's absurd. I've lived like everybody else" (p. 9). The reader has enough information to know that the narrator has not lived as described. The development of the story will show the untruth of his denial of being a dreamer.

Thus, before starting into the series of dreams to be related by Linacero, the reader should be aware that he cannot take the declarations and judgments of the narrator at face value but must instead search for evidence of other interpretations. Without this realization it would be impossible to interpret the relation of Eladio to the prostitute Ester, or to see the self-knowledge she forces on him, or to recognize his methods of evasion. If the scene with Ester were not interpreted correctly, Linacero's final state of desperation would be deprived of much of its meaning, because it then would not be greatly different from his state at the beginning.

As a literary device the deceitful narrator poses several problems. First of all, the reader must not have a sense of being manipulated by the author. Onetti avoids this problem by making deceit an integral part of the narrator's character and an essential part of the meaning of that which is narrated.

In terms of personality, Linacero's deceit becomes an external measure of his alienation. He can tell the reader about his solitude and isolation from humanity, but only through the discovery of his deceit is the reader able to judge Linacero's alienation from himself and his inability to exercise self-control even in an artistic creation.

Another problem is the possibility of excessive distancing of the reader from the character, with resultant loss of interest in the entire work. This possibility is also avoided because the detection and evaluation of the deceit become a necessity. Thus, although the reader is separated from the protagonist, he participates in the work because of the independent judgments he has to make.

Onetti uses the deceitful narrator, with significant variations, in other works. In *La cara de la desgracia* the reader, because of events, must decide if the narrator is telling the truth, but he must do so without any conclusive textual evidence. The meaning of the story changes completely, according to his decision. *Para una tumba sin nombre* has two narrators. The admission of deceit by one of them, Jorge Malabia, is made totally ambiguous because of conflicting lies by several persons.

A new dimension of Linacero's alienation is presented when he starts to tell what happened with Ana María. He places the adventure in the world of real events, "something that happened in the real world . . ." (p. 9). This description of course implies a split emotional life, and it is the first evidence of a divided personality. Three of the narrated episodes—with Ana María, with Ester the prostitute, and with his wife—revolve around the relation between his dream world and the real world. It becomes apparent that the only satisfactory life he has takes place in his dream world. His attempts at communication fail because people either reject his dream world or see the true motives behind it that he is unwilling to accept. The division is so important that it is reflected by the novel's imagery. Each world is characterized by its way of looking at people and objects. Thus the description of the episode with Ana María is worthy of special attention for what it reveals about the "real world" and its relation to the imaginary one.

The first aspect of interest in this episode is another contra-
diction. It reaffirms the falsity of Linacero's denial of being a
dreamer and his claim of having led a normal life. He says of his
adolescence, "Even then I had nothing to do with anyone" (p.
10). This statement extends his solitude and alienation into
childhood and suggests causes other than the philosophical rejection of the world implied in his introduction and presented
again when he describes his failure with other people. It seems
legitimate to infer the existence of the same irrational disgust
with and rejection of life in adolescence that is present in Linacero's adulthood, as one can deduce from his reaction to the view
from his room.

Two other features of the encounter with Ana María deserve
attention. The first is the way she is described, and the second is
the sexual content of the episode, both manifest and latent, and
its relation to the dream of Ana María and "the log cabin."

When Linacero portrays Ana María, he describes only parts of
her body: her arm, shoulder, and neck. He recognizes her "by
her way of carrying an arm separated from her body" (p. 10).
When he looks at her he sees only "nude arms and the nape of
her neck" (p. 11). When he attacks Ana María he uses the same
fragmented form of description. Her rage is shown by her
breasts. "Only her chest, her huge breasts, were moving, desperate with rage and fatigue" (p. 12). Never is there any kind of
description that allows a total vision of the girl.

It is obvious that the assault is sexual and yet Linacero dis-
claims any desire. "I never had, at any moment, the intention of
violating her; I had no desire for her" (p. 12). However, he gives
no reason for his actions, only indirectly suggesting a wish to
humiliate. In his description, nevertheless, it is he who is humiliated. It seems reasonable to assume, given his age, that what he
narrates is his sexual initiation and that, due to failure, humili-
ation, or totally unexplained reasons, he does not wish to, or
cannot, reveal the true nature of the encounter.

Linacero's sexual desires toward Ana María do not become
manifest until he describes the dream based on the encounter in

real life. As a prologue to the dream he relates its content to Ana María in the "real world." "But now I don't have to lay stupid traps. She is the one who comes at night, without my calling her, without knowing where she comes from . . . Nude, she extends herself on the burlap covering of the bough bed" (p. 14). Sex is the only motive in the dream, but the initiative has been transferred to Ana María. Furthermore, the Eladio Linacero she offers herself to has no relation either to the adolescent who desired her but hid his desire from himself or to the solitary, alienated, withdrawn man writing in his room. The imagined Linacero is a gregarious man of action, the object of unreasoned sexual desire. Thus in both dream and reality Linacero presents a distorted image of himself. In the dream the image is changed by fantasy that would seem to be compensatory for an unacceptable reality. In reality it is changed by omission or misdirection in order to conceal his true nature and feelings from himself. In both cases the projected self-image indicates the irrational basis of his alienation.

Thus one aspect of Angel Rama's description of the function of dreams seems to be incorrect. He states, "If there is a dominant and original line running through the story, defining it, defining the character, it is this capacity for 'dreaming,' removing himself from reality."[16] At all levels of narration Linacero alters reality. The difference between the dreams and the "real world" lies in the method and degree of separation from reality, not in the separation itself.

Another major difference exists between Linacero's dreams and all other events. The fragmented vision resulting in incomplete images in his description of the real Ana María has already been noted. In the dream this type of vision is absent. Instead Linacero gives a complete description of Ana María's body. "From above, without gesture and without speaking to her, I look at her cheeks that are starting to flush, at the thousand drops shining on her body and moving with the flames of the fire, at her breasts that seem to quiver like a flickering candle agitated by silent steps. The girl's face has an open frank look,

and, scarcely separating her lips, she smiles at me" (pp. 14–15).
The part of the body he isolates indicates his desire. "Slowly, still
looking at her, I sit on the edge of the bed and fix my eyes on the
black triangle, still shining from the storm. It is then, exactly, that
the adventure begins" (p. 15). The sexual aspect of Linacero's
fragmented vision is perfectly clear. When he is attempting to
conceal his desire from himself and the reader, he fragments the
body and describes parts that generally have no sexual interest.
In the fantasized dream, where his desire is foremost, the body
and its sexual attributes are completely described.

A point of coincidence between dreams and reality is seen
when Linacero, after speaking about a woman with whom he has
had sexual relations, generalizes about women. "A woman will be
eternally closed to one, in spite of everything, if one does not
possess her with the spirit of a violator" (p. 17). This is a projection of a wish from his dream world into the real world. Only
in the former is he a man of action, a "violator." This projection
shows, again, the confusion of self-image between dream world
and real world. It also perhaps reveals a hidden wish not to communicate with women, as this concept of physical love precludes
communication. A further indication of this desire appears when
Hanka asks Linacero a question—why he thinks that he will
never fall in love again—that to answer would require both communication and self-realization. Rather than respond he breaks
his relation with her. In addition, his philosophical outlook toward both women and humanity in general radically changes.
Significantly, he rejects the possibility of communication with
women, allowing a good deal of hate and disgust to show. "Why,
a few lines before, was I speaking of understanding? None of
these filthy beasts are able to understand anything" (p. 19). In
the same fashion he shows his basic dislike of humanity: ". . . but
the truth is that there are no people like that, healthy as animals.
There are only men and women who are animals" (p. 18). Both
of these statements are a long way from the earlier viewpoints
expressed, but they are more revealing of the truth of Linacero's

nature in that they come in response to stimuli that activate the deeper levels of his being. What is now completely visible is an all-encompassing disgust toward life and other human beings.

Of the additional attempts at communication described by Linacero only one is central to further understanding of his character and alienation. The others—with his former wife and with Cordes—add to his frustration and push him toward partial self-realization and desolation. In his relation with Ester, the prostitute, he is forced to look at the real, and probably most important, function of his dreams. Angel Rama has described this function: "The pleasurable, erotic, content of these dreams is known; it nourishes the masturbatory episodes . . ."[17] Rama does not, however, deal with the importance of Linacero's being confronted with this knowledge, beyond recognizing his rejection of the charge by the prostitute.

There is a great deal of similarity, in terms of structure and imagery, between Linacero's description of his relation with the prostitute and the earlier episode with Ana María. The reader again sees something that takes place in the "real world." After failure on this plane there is a dream, much abbreviated as compared to the one of "the log cabin," that changes the reality involved. The description of Ester is another example of fragmented vision. "But she seemed younger, and her arms, thick and white, stretched out, milky in the light of the café, as if, on sinking into life, she had raised her hands, desperately pleading for help, thrashing like a drowned person, and the arms had remained behind, distant in time, the arms of a young girl, separate from the large nervous body, which no longer existed" (p. 20). The same process is at work but in a more exaggerated fashion. Not only do the parts of the prostitute described have no sexual connotations, but also they are surprisingly related to an earlier state of purity. That this difficult association takes place due to emotional needs of the narrator is obvious, because it is totally divorced from the physical and emotional reality of the situation. Linacero again seems to be masking his sexual desires as he did

in the description of his assault on Ana María. His wish not to
pay Ester can be interpreted as a symptom of his evasion, in that
the money would be an open declaration of sexual intent.

It is also significant that Linacero interrupts the narrative of
the lowest point in his life, the sexual conquest of a whore, to talk
about the highest point, his brief love for his former wife. He
says, "There had been something marvelous created by us" (p.
22). He offers two generalities to cover the failure of love and his
marriage. "Love is marvelous and absurd, and, incomprehen-
sibly, it touches all classes of souls. But absurd marvelous people
are rare, and they are that way only for a short time, in early
youth. Afterward they begin to accept, and they are lost" (p.
23). The basic belief expressed here is in the destructive power
of life and of experience. The state of purity referred to can exist
only in early youth, when there has been no exposure to life and
no adjustment of ideals to reality. Youth is also the time of sexual
awakening. It is this awakening that lies behind the other generalization, which is again overlaid by the idea of a lost purity.
"And if one marries a girl and one day wakes at the side of a
woman, it is possible that one will understand, without disgust,
the souls of violators of children and the drooling kindness of
those old men who wait with chocolates at school street corners"
(p. 23). Here, however, the only attraction of youth is sexual.

The idea of purity is the key to the explanation of the episode
with Ester. After succeeding in going with her to a hotel without
paying, Linacero attempts to talk to her, when she is dressing,
about her dreams and to create one for her. She responds with
disgust, telling him that she knows they serve as an introduction
to masturbation. He does not deny the charge; instead, as he did
with Hanka, he rejects the person. "She was a wretched woman,
and it was imbecilic to speak to her about this" (p. 27). He converts her into a dream, where she becomes completely pure and
innocent. "At times I think about her, and there is an adventure
in which Ester comes to visit me, or we unexpectedly meet, drinking and talking as good friends. She then tells me the things she
dreams or imagines and they are always things of extraordinary

purity, as simple as tales for children" (p. 27). The major modification is that she, in what she communicates as a dreamer, has
taken over the role of Linacero. By giving her purity he has given
it to himself. The inference is that the disgust felt by Ester was
also felt by Linacero, and what he is trying to conceal is self-hate.

This interpretation is indirectly supported by the beginning of
the paragraph following the one quoted above. Onetti uses a
habitual action that has already acquired meaning to indicate the
hidden reaction of Linacero. "I don't know what time it is. I've
smoked so much that tobacco disgusts me" (p. 27). His definition
of his essential life is that he is a solitary man who smokes. Re-
pugnance for smoking symbolically means disgust with self and
with life.

In addition to the indirect evidence discussed above, the last
two episodes show a growing awareness on Linacero's part of his
own self-hate. It is revealed directly but gradually. The first stage
occurs when his roommate calls him a failure. Linacero only suggests his reaction. "But Lázaro doesn't know what he's saying
when he screams 'failure' at me. He can't even suspect what that
word means to me" (p. 29). Nevertheless, he does not expand on
its meaning for him, instead making the reader guess what it
might be. To be sensitive to failure can only indicate insecurity
in terms of self-image and self-esteem.

In the episode with Cordes, Linacero for the first time in his
narrative expresses a feeling of happiness and a belief that he is
communicating. "It has been a long time since I felt so happy,
free, talking with enthusiasm, tumultuously, without vacillation,
sure of being understood, also listening with the same intensity,
trying to foresee Cordes's thoughts" (p. 32). He tells Cordes a
fantastic dream, and when he is not understood he has a violent
reaction. "I'm sick of everything, do you understand, of people,
of life, of proper verse. I go in a corner and imagine all that. That
and dirty things, every night" (p. 34). This is at last the truth
about himself, and its intensity can be explained only by the unwilling increase in self-awareness that has taken place through
the narrative. Because of it he is partially able to assess his posi-

tion in respect to himself and to others. His new perspective becomes evident when he compares himself to Lázaro, his roommate, for whom he has shown only disgust. "When all's said and done it's he who is the poet and dreamer. I'm a miserable man who turns at night toward the shadowed wall to think shoddy fantastic things" (p. 35).

Linacero's final statement about life carries the entire weight of the anguish that gradually reveals itself in the narrative. "This is night; he who couldn't feel it doesn't know it. Everything in life is shit, and now we're blind in the night, attentive and without comprehension" (p. 35). It is evident that, although he faces his condition more fully than before, he does not totally accept it and still desires communication with other human beings. It is a one-sided act of communication to extend, by the use of the first person plural, his condition onto humanity.

The picture of alienation that has emerged from the study of what the narrator relates and what can be seen behind his words is one of almost total withdrawal and isolation, made even more intense by repeated efforts at communication. The underlying causes of this alienation are rooted in the character of the narrator and are not due to any outside social pressures. The essence of Linacero's personality is an irrational disgust for all aspects of living. This disgust is coupled with self-hate that seems to arise from his adult sexual life. However, the origins of these features remain largely conjectural. Onetti has limited himself to presenting the condition without going into the causes of it.

The dominant technique used in the development of the protagonist's personality is that of the deceitful narrator. The reader, although distanced from Linacero, participates in the work because he has to make judgments about it that affect the meaning of the entire story.

Two other techniques were noted. One, the use of habitual or repeated action, does not play a very great role in *El pozo*, although several times the act of smoking carries the true meaning of what is being narrated. Of much more importance are the vision and visual images described by the narrator. A fragmented imagery is characteristic of all that he describes in the real world. The dream world contains coherent vision and imagery. The sexual aspect of this vision has been discussed, but its relation to the personality of Linacero was only indirectly dwelt upon. He obviously has a totally split personality in that his emotional life takes place in his imaginary world. His external "real world" personality is permeated by his fantasy self. Neither part functions satisfactorily. The visual fragmentation is schizophrenic, offering a broken surface with no depth coherence. An example of this depthless vision is the lack of sexual connotations of the parts of the female body described in the "real world." Only in the fantasy world is there something behind the imagery.[18]

Thus, in order to convey the experience of extreme alienation, Onetti has created a schizoid form of vision and made it coincide with the split personality of the protagonist. On a different plane he has fragmented normal action patterns, emphasizing repeated or habitual actions. The result of this technique is to give the entire work a schizoid atmosphere. The personality of the protagonist is, however, the determinant for the techniques used to create alienation. This is not the case in many of the later works of Onetti, in which the personality becomes lost in a web of objects, actions, incongruous emotions, and partially understood symbolism. *Tan triste como ella* will be seen to contain many of these features.

In addition to the other planes of imagery, there is a symbolic plane in *El pozo*, but it is weakly developed and serves only as background to the narrative. All the important action, real and imaginary, takes place in small enclosed areas. On the real plane this setting is indicative of the isolation of the protagonist, but in the imaginary world these enclosed areas, "the log cabin," above all, become indistinct sexual symbols. All the imagery related to the cabin has sexual overtones on an oneiric Freudian level.

The theme of artistic creation introduced at the beginning of *El pozo* is seen to be determined and formed by the personality of the narrator. The content of his dreams is a manifestation of emotions and desires that he conceals from himself in the real world. The dreams also serve as sexual stimulants. The reader is able to judge the extent of alienation by the schizoid form it forces upon the images and actions of the protagonist. In contrast to this process of creation of imagery from within the person, in the next work to be studied, *Tan triste como ella*, the images come from outside the protagonist and are projected inward.

Tan triste como ella was published in 1963 and therefore must be considered among the mature works of Onetti. Emir Rodríguez Monegal believes that the first part of Onetti's writing, from *El pozo* to *La vida breve*, is a documental cycle.[19] Mario Benedetti defines Onetti's attitude at the close of this cycle: "Emir Rodríguez Monegal has shown that *La vida breve* closes, in a certain sense, that documental cycle opened ten years before by *El pozo*. The cycle is closed, effectively, but with a semiconfession of impotence or, better, of impossibility: being cannot fuse with the world; it does not succeed in blending with life. From this deficiency another path paradoxically opens, another possibility: the protagonist creates an imaginary being that blends with his being and into whose being he can blend."[20] *Tan triste* was chosen for this study because it is the clearest statement in Onetti's writing of man's radical inability to penetrate life and to communicate with other human beings. It shows what Onetti's characters do when there is no evasion, only struggle with their crushing concept of reality. Their alienation is clear and total.

Tan triste is also the most symbolic of all Onetti's works. Many of them can be interpreted symbolically, the best example being *El astillero*. In this novel both the action and the situation have strong symbolic overtones. In *Tan triste* there is a profusion of objects and actions that have only symbolic meaning and that impinge upon the protagonist. It will be seen that the symbolism of *Tan triste*, like that of the images in *El pozo*, is of a special nature to meet the needs of the author in his expression of extreme alienation.

The outstanding difference between *El pozo* and *Tan triste como ella* is the latter novel's complexity. While in *El pozo* ambiguity is restricted to the true motives of the protagonist, in *Tan triste* it extends to all aspects of the work: its structure, symbolism, and meaning.

In broad outline the novel has a cyclic structure, beginning and ending with the same image. The first part is a symbolic dream that at the end becomes reality with the suicide of the female protagonist. Emir Rodríguez Monegal has described the structural function of the image: "In the girl's form of suicide there is a very clear reference to her first contact with the protagonist, so that the beginning and end of the long story are unified with the same image, creating a completely closed and cyclic universe, a universe of indubitable phallic obsession."[21] However, to characterize the world as one of phallic obsession is an oversimplification. The obsession is sexual. It will be seen that almost all the symbols are sexual, but only a part of them are phallic. The symbolic meaning of the form of suicide is definitely phallic, but too much emphasis should not be put on it by itself.

At the level of action, very little takes place in the novel, which is the examination of a marriage in the last stages of disintegration. The focus is the woman, whose personal collapse matches that of the marriage. Her husband brings in well-diggers to destroy the garden of the house. The woman watches them work, seduces two of them, has during the period of the novel ritual combats with the vegetation of the garden, and at last commits suicide. The disconnected nature of the events indicates that the meaning and movement of the novel are to be found elsewhere. The emotional life of the protagonist is the center of the work. The novel follows her through several moments of discovery that lead to increased despair and to suicide.

Another feature of *Tan triste como ella* that distinguishes it from most of Onetti's other novels is the presence of the author. Onetti's most common technique is the use of multiple narrators, one of the functions of which is to completely mask the presence and thoughts of the author. In *Para una tumba sin nombre*, for example, Díaz Grey is the narrator, but the story is about what he is told by Jorge Malabia. This structure is further complicated by a third narrator, Tito, who casts doubt on the veracity of the entire story. In this confusion the reader entirely loses sight of the thoughts and attitudes of the author, and anything he infers about them is overlaid by three levels of narration. The same process is seen in *El pozo*, in a more simplified form. Because of the protagonist's deceit, the reader's entire effort is directed toward understanding him and does not seek beyond the character for the author's attitudes. This aspect would not be important if the artistic goal were to create autonomous characters instead of "intensities of life." Onetti's figures are openly manipulated, either by the narrator-character or by the reader himself, because of the choices he must make about their actions and motives. The lack of the author's presence thus has to be significant. It is a form of alienation, a desire not to be responsible for or to have lasting visible control over one's actions. Many critics have assumed that the narrator's viewpoint is also that of Onetti. This assumption seems to be supported by the uniformity of tone throughout. However, the deception or ambiguity characteristic of these narrators indicates the need for additional evidence before any view can be assigned to the author. *Tan triste* provides some of this evidence.

The reader is made aware of Onetti's presence before the work begins by an introductory letter whose outstanding characteristics are ambiguity and evasion. The letter is to "Tantriste," and there is no indication if Onetti is addressing a person or, as an artist, his creation. The terms are predominantly personal; the time has come to break an intimacy and to separate. There is a declaration of mutual alienation and defeat. "I don't believe we ever truly understood each other; I accept my guilt, the blame, the responsibility, and the failure."[22] This declaration is immediately followed by a retreat from the personal position toward what seems to be a literary one. "I intend to apologize—only for us, however—invoking the difficulty caused by beating around the bush for X pages" (p. 135). However, the meaning of this statement is also equivocal because there is no relevant context for the phrase "beating around the bush." The last line is again personal, another statement of isolation and alienation. "I never looked you in the face, I never showed you mine" (p. 135). It is also, in whatever context, a declaration of evasion and of a desire to keep the self hidden.

The letter, then, offers a problem of interpretation. There is no conclusive evidence for either of two possibilities: the letter could represent a personal or a literary position. Because both seem to be valid they must be accepted, and the letter itself, as has been shown, places them together within the same sentence. Both possibilities express alienation in the form of radical solitude, evasion, and withdrawal. But, because of the ambiguity, it is impossible to make any inference as to the extent of the author's personal revelation.

Another aspect of the ambiguity of the letter deserves attention. The uncertainty as to meaning is coupled with vague references to actual events, "the intimacy of the last few months," "the failure," and "the happy moments." The effect, implied certainty joined to ambiguity, destroys any deep meaning. The emotions presented suggest a depth of feeling that is vitiated by the form. The result is an emotional surface with nothing behind it. The emotional experience arising from this depthless surface is schizoid in nature.

Tan triste begins with a description of a past involving the main figures before they were married. The tone is similar to that of the introductory letter. "She wanted to go, she wanted something to happen, the most brutal thing, the most anemic and deceiving—anything helpful to her solitude and her ignorance. She was not thinking about the future and felt capable of denying it. But a fear that had nothing to do with the old pain made her say no, defending herself with her hands and with the rigidity of her muscles. She only obtained, accepted, the taste of the man stained by the sun and the beach" (p. 137). The action is minimal and nebulous, a frustrated sexual attempt. The emotional life of the woman is the subject of the paragraph, but the outlines of that too are lost in ambiguity. Her isolation from life is clear, as is her desire for it in any form. Her emotional reaction to the man's

sexual advances is described in terms that have no meaning. Her
fear has no origin, and there is not the slightest indication as to
what "the old pain" means. Neither does the compromise, "the
taste of the man," make sense. Only after the symbolic sexual
meaning of the final act of suicide is determined does this phrase
become clear. As will be seen later, the hidden content here is the
sexual initiation of the woman through an act of perversion.

The initial reaction of the reader to the scene is the same as his
reaction to the letter. There is an emotional surface that suggests
depth but that on examination is seen to cover nothing.

The woman's dream that follows the opening scene is rich in
imagery. As has already been pointed out, both the dream and its
images have structural importance in that they define the closed
world of the story. They also have symbolic importance at several
different levels. The first and most obvious is as a foreshadowing
of the course of the novel in oneiric terms. "She dreamed, at
dawn, already separate and distant, that she was traveling alone
in a night that could have been another, almost nude in her short
chemise, carrying an empty suitcase. She was condemned to desperation and was dragging her bare feet along the tree-lined
street, slowly, her body upright, almost defiant" (p. 137). The
visible comment on the protagonist's condition is presented
through straightforward rational symbolism; she is in a labyrinth,
condemned to despair. Her emotional state is not connected to
the imagery of the dream but is instead described by the author.
A second level of symbolism present is irrational in nature: "the
empty suitcase." The suitcase is associated with her nudity. As-
suming that this is a true oneiric element, one can apply the prin-
ciples of dream analysis. The symbol is sexual and must mask
unacceptable emotions. As a concrete element it would seem to
symbolize the emptiness of the protagonist's sexual life. This interpretation is borne out by her actions during the course of the
novel, by the failure of her sexual liaisons.

As the dream continues, it maintains the division between the
author's intellectual descriptions and oneiric irrational imagery,
as is shown by the following description: "The disillusionment,

the sadness, the having to say yes to death, could be borne only because, capriciously, the taste of the man was reborn in her throat at each intersection when she asked for and ordered it" (p. 137). Here, however, the irrational aspect, "taste of the man," refers to the first scene, where its meaning is also completely ambiguous.

The last part of the dream continues with the same blend of rational commentary and irrational imagery. "Step by step, she realized that she was not advancing with the suitcase toward any destiny, any bed, any room. Almost nude, with her body straight and her breasts piercing the night, she went on walking to immerse herself in the disproportionate moon that kept growing" (p. 138). An emotional state is again described and coupled with an ambiguous action. The moon as an image can have many meanings. In the context of the dream only a generalized interpretation is possible, due to lack of corroborative elements. The moon in some way symbolizes an abdication or destruction of personality. This interpretation is verified at the end of the novel by the repetition of these same lines to describe the suicide of the protagonist.

Within the dream, then, there is a two-level presentation of the woman's alienation. On the rational plane her solitude and despair are visible. The more complex irrational level symbolically presents her own attitude toward her body, in sexual terms. She is divorced from her feminine sexuality, for reasons unknown, and, more importantly, she seems to be self-destructive. The dream could be viewed as a fulfillment of a death wish in light of its connection with her suicide at the end of the novel.

The protagonist's alienation, then, is total at the beginning of the novel. The symbolic message of the dream also has a structural function in outlining the trajectory of the protagonist from despair to destruction. *El pozo*, starting at the same emotional point, ends in the protagonist's desolation without self-destruction. In *Tan triste*, by the elimination of the first-person narration, the despair, desolation, and destruction seen at the end of the work are generalized into the human condition.

The failure of the marriage is presented first from the masculine viewpoint and is due to the same reasons found in *El pozo*: inevitable loss of innocence and transformation from girl to woman. "He had loved the small woman who prepared his food, who had given birth to a creature that cried incessantly on the second floor. Now he regarded her with surprise; she was, fleetingly, something worse, shorter, deader than some unknown woman whose name never comes to us" (p. 139). This attitude, because of its persistence through all of Onetti's work, can certainly be considered as a basic attribute of the author. He does not deny the existence of human happiness through love. Instead, he believes in the inevitability of a transformation into unhappiness because of the nature of life. The emotional result of the form of this belief, a movement from positive to negative, assures a maximum degree of suffering both for those who undergo the experience and for those who believe it is a fundamental truth. In terms of alienation and loss of self the view has several functions. It can be a defense of the alienated, withdrawn individual in that it provides a reason not to participate in life. It can also be a symptom of an extensive dislocation of self through self-hate. The person who hates himself, as does Eladio Linacero, frequently punishes himself. Linacero's attempts at communication are a form of self-punishment. Another form, seen in many of Onetti's characters, is the adherence to a pain-causing belief.

The husband in *Tan triste como ella* is resigned to the pain of living: ". . . and the years, thirty-two of them, taught him, at least, the uselessness of all abandon, of all hope of understanding" (p. 138). At the time of the novel he defends himself against his anguish by searching for other women and by drinking. His emotional state and the activities around it remain constant throughout the novel and serve to push his wife into complete alienation. She goes through several stages in her reactions to his activities, which touch her on two levels, emotional and symbolic. At first she wants to share her unhappiness with him: ". . . for a while she tried to understand without contempt; she wanted to come near him with part of the pity she felt for herself, for life and its end"

(p. 141). When these attempts fail she undergoes the first of a series of emotional changes. "In the middle of September, imperceptibly at first, the woman began to find comfort, to believe that life is like a mountain or a rock, that we didn't make it, that neither the one or the other made it" (p. 141). This is a mildly alienated viewpoint in that it implies a separation of the self from life and from its own actions within life, but it is a tenable position. For Onetti it is the start of the protagonist's descent to suicide and the real beginning of the novel, which he indicates by his own presence, using the first person plural: ". . . what we are trying to relate began on a quiet autumn afternoon . . ." (p. 141). It immediately becomes obvious that the focus of the novel is going to be a symbolic struggle between husband and wife, rather than the increasing separation that accompanies it. The pivotal element in the struggle is the garden.

At first the garden seems to be only a symbol of early innocence that offered the girl protection from the world. "And when the world came searching for her she didn't completely understand, protected and deceived by the capricious and ill-kept shrubs, by the mystery—in light and shadow—of the old trees, twisted and intact, by the innocent grass, tall and coarse" (p. 142). The man's desire is ostensibly to destroy this refuge. "A corner to stretch out in, where, when summer comes, one can have cool drinks, can remain, near the big windows. But the rest, all of it, has to be covered with cement. I want to make fish tanks" (p. 143).

This level of meaning is reinforced by Onetti's description of the woman's attitude toward the relation between herself and the garden: ". . . that she didn't believe possible the vengeance, the destruction of the garden and her own life" (p. 144). There is a parallel between the destruction of the garden and the disintegration of the woman's life. At the obvious symbolic level discussed above of husband against wife, their relationship deteriorates as the garden disappears. The setting for this deterioration has already been briefly described; both husband and wife believe only in unhappiness as the inevitable result of living. The man does not see any possibility of happiness with the woman his wife has become and looks to the past to remember it. "He, on the other hand, was waiting for the miracle, the resurrection of the pregnant girl he had known, his own, the girl of the love they believed in or were creating for months, with resolution, without deliberate deceit, abandoned so close to happiness" (p. 146).

His wife's attitude is more complex and is tied into the series of discoveries she makes during the process of the novel. "She believed she knew something more, she thought about destiny, about mistakes and mysteries, she accepted the guilt and—at the end—finally admitted that to live is sufficient guilt so that we should accept the pay, recompense, or punishment. The same thing, when all is said and done" (p. 145).

Several features of this quotation are of interest. Foremost is the presence of the author indicated by the first person plural. Its limited use, however, makes the extent of his agreement with what is expressed ambiguous and would seem to be a form of evasion. The underlying attitude is again disgust with life. This belief could be that of Eladio Linacero in *El pozo*. All Onetti's main characters share this view. Only Larsen in *El astillero*, because of his desire to endure despite misfortune, seems to have found something positive and irreducible at the corrupt core of life. But because of the persistence and pervasiveness of this disgust with life in all of Onetti's writing it must be considered as a basic element of his personality. Its context, as has been shown, is always that of evasion and ambiguity, and its existence must frequently be deduced from secondary evidence. Thus it is essentially an emotional perspective rather than an articulated philosophical stance. It is the medium in which Onetti and his characters live rather than the meaning of their existence. Their reaction to it is essentially that of irrational evasion. Linacero creates dreams that cover his radical revulsion toward life and himself. Brausen creates entire worlds in which he can find some meaning or satisfaction. Díaz Grey observes and speculates, seeing an endless series of equally valid possibilities in most human situations.

The ambiguity of the forms that life takes with this view as its point of departure is another feature seen in the lines quoted. For the sin of living one receives either "pay, recompense, or punishment," but they are all the same and have no separate meaning. The root of this ambiguity is alienation. If life is viewed with repulsion, the viewer is already radically separate from it, and whatever forms it assumes are equally distant from the nonparticipating self.

As her marriage collapses, the woman in *Tan triste* moves toward a confrontation with her disgust with life. Her discovery of her husband's infidelity and his destruction of the life of a former friend, Mendel, who meant nothing to her, are the external events that lead to the confrontation. Accompanying this movement is an increasing complexity of symbolism surrounding the garden and its destruction. As more symbolic levels come into existence, the ambiguity surrounding their meaning increases.

This increasing ambiguity is seen with the introduction of a series of new elements. The first is totally ambiguous and yet eventually becomes the central image in the protagonist's descent to suicide. The woman has taken to watching the workmen in the garden. "She sniffed the air, she was waiting for the solitude of five in the afternoon, the daily ritual, the conquered absurdity, made almost a habit" (p. 147). At this point the description has no meaning. Nothing is known of "the ritual" or of the fact that it has become almost a habit. Yet, at the end of the novel when she can no longer participate in the ritual, the woman kills herself. Thus, because of the manner of introduction, the ambiguity surrounding this action is intentional. Juxtaposed with this unclear description is a more concrete image: "First there was the incomprehensible excitement of the well itself, the black hole sinking in the earth. It would have been enough. But she soon discovered, at the bottom, the pair of men working, with nude torsos" (p. 147). The meaning, however, is again ambiguous. The first impression is that there is an excess of emotion for the object contemplated. The key to the image does not come until later in the novel, when the woman has sexual intercourse with the well-diggers. In retrospect the image of the men in the well becomes symbolic of the act of sexual intercourse. This interpretation is verified by a repetition of the image when the woman approaches the first well-digger. The sexual connotations are obvious. "She was decided, sure now that it was inevitable, suspecting that she had wanted it from the moment she saw the well and, inside, the torso of the man digging" (p. 155). It is important to note that the well is a feminine sexual symbol.

Once the sexual connotations of the imagery are established Onetti returns to what will be the central image in the novel, the woman's ritual that he had left undescribed. "But she chose without conviction, without true desire, the useless and bloody game with the Jerusalem thorns, against them, plants or trees. She sought, for no reason, to no end, to open a path among the trunks and the spines. She panted for a while, tearing her hands. She always ended in failure, accepting it, saying yes with a grimace, a smile" (p. 149). The absence of logical meaning for the struggle and its apparent lack of relation to any previous action or thought of the protagonist limit its significance to the symbolic plane. The ritual nature of the struggle has already been indicated by Onetti. The struggle's elements—thorns, spines, and so on—are clearly phallic. The only value that can be attached to the garden as a whole, based on its immediate context, is that of some sort of a labyrinth.

The sexual nature of the garden is made clear by two bits of evidence immediately related to it. The lines quoted are juxtaposed in the text with an obvious symbol of sexual intercourse, the well-digger in the well, the connotations of which extend over a large part of the novel. Also there is the phrase, "saying yes," which makes no sense within the quotation. However, its opposite occurs in the first paragraph of the novel as a rejection of intercourse: "But a fear that had nothing to do with the old pain made her say no . . ." (p. 137). In broader terms the garden is the feminine side of the struggle with the husband. He wishes to destroy it with a masculine sexual symbol, cement. Thus the garden seems to be an ambiguous symbol for feminine sexuality in conflict with masculine sexuality. Nevertheless, although the symbol's general nature is moderately clear, its meaning for the woman and her struggle with it are not. Even the additional information that the garden has provided the only true happiness the woman has known since infancy, and that the husband discovered in it the only thing that was of true importance to her, seems to be unimportant. However, if one considers that the novel is built around total sexual polarization, as is indicated by all its symbolism, then two possibilities suggest themselves. The first is that, because of the garden's importance in the woman's youth, the feminine sexuality it represents is that which is uncontaminated by contact with masculinity. Onetti's interest in and repetition of the theme of the loss of purity and the loss of virginity would tend to support this interpretation. The other possibility is that the symbolic pleasure resulting from the struggle with the garden is erotic. In the context of a completely feminine sexuality this pleasure would mean symbolic masturbation. Again, either masturbation or autostimulation is a theme seen in Onetti's work. It is important in *El pozo*. In all cases it results in self-punishment and self-disgust. The fact that as the garden is destroyed the woman turns to promiscuous sexual activity with the men who are physically destroying it would give some support to this interpretation. The central feature is, however, that because of lack of direct evidence and due to intentional ambiguity the meaning of the symbol remains conjectural. The result is a fragmentation of imagery on a deeper level than has been seen in other works by Onetti. Surface fragmentation is evident in *El pozo*, with a consequent lack of depth. In this central image in *Tan triste* the vertical dimension of the fragmentation is greatly extended. There is neither rational nor irrational, conscious nor subconscious coherence. This is not to say that Onetti has abandoned the techniques seen in *El pozo*. The broken surface imagery is evident in the description of the well-diggers, where only parts of their bodies—their arms and chests—are described. The only total presentation of a human body occurs in the woman's dream. These techniques are merely extended into areas where they were not seen before.

The form and nature of the woman's alienation are directly related to the symbolic presentation of the conflicts that drive her to suicide. That she experiences these conflicts symbolically is the measure of the separation of her self from direct experience. In addition the ambiguity of the nature of the conflicts reflects the fragmentation of the self. She is estranged from her body and in conflict over the nature of her sexuality. Heterosexual activity in the form that she has known it is a threat to her personality. This fact is evident in her relation to her child, who should be regarded as a fulfillment of married sexual life. Instead she hates him for being male and shows absolutely no emotional bond with him. She expresses the wish for a female child, who would have been an affirmation of her flawed sexuality and could not be related to the masculine threat she fears.

The rest of the novel is mainly concerned with the emotional trajectory of the woman and reveals more of her alienation. After the scene in the garden she has a major change in emotional orientation, caused by a line she discovers in a book: "Imagine the growing sorrow, the desire to flee, the impotent disgust, the submission, the hate" (p. 153). Externally this line describes her marriage and her relation to her husband: separation, anger, and hate. When the same sentence is used at the end, just before she commits suicide, it describes her attitude toward life. Several important events take place in between. Hating her husband and knowing he has a mistress who gives him some degree of happiness, she retaliates by sexual involvement with the well-diggers. Her reaction to the first well-digger as he comes toward her, nude, is of great importance. "Now she watched him approach and began to realize her hate for the other's physical superiority, for everything masculine, for him who commands, for him who doesn't have to ask useless questions" (p. 157). The man is impotent and the effort is a failure. Its nature is, however, clearly self-destructive; the woman is submitting to something she hates for reasons that are not clear. The act only increases her loss of self.

Before she initiates relations with the second laborer her relationship with her husband is divested of any possibility of fulfillment. He tells her that he loved the girl she used to be but that love has disappeared because of "so much cunning and dissimulation and treachery" (p. 161). In Onetti's world this is more than a personal failure between two people. It is the failure of life itself and has no remedy. As has been seen, experience and age destroy love and innocence. This is the level on which the woman accepts the failure. Her seduction of the second laborer is the penultimate act of her struggle against life. The terms of its failure are explicit. "But, inevitably and slowly, the woman had to come back from desperate sexuality to the need for love" (p. 163). This sentence also defines another aspect of her alienation. Her self is incomplete and split because she has separated sex from emotion. She needs the latter in the form of love, but the process of life denies it to her, and the former, because of her imperfect sexuality, is self-destructive.

As the novel nears its end the symbolic plane comes to the foreground. The reasons for the woman's suicide are presented entirely in this plane. The major element that pushes her toward self-destruction is the failure of the ritual in the garden. "The thorns no longer had the strength to wound and they dripped, barely, milk, a slow and viscous liquid, whitish, lazy. She tried other trunks and all were the same, manageable, inoffensive, oozing" (p. 164). The symbolic meaning is clear; the milk and the cement that covered the garden are related elements of masculine sexuality that have destroyed the garden, the symbol of the woman's uncontaminated femininity. Her reaction to the loss of the garden shows that her self has also been destroyed. She no longer has any contact with reality, and her actions are completely separate from her. "Everything was a game, a rite, a prologue" (p. 154).

In preparation for her suicide she relives the moment of her sexual awakening: ". . . she slid until she fell on the bed, she reconstructed the first time and had to lose control, to cry, to see again that night's moon, surrendered, like a child" (p. 164). The moment's nature and form, like those of all crucial actions in *Tan*

triste, are ambiguous. There is no definite indication as to
whether it is heterosexual or homosexual, but the manner of description and the emotional response seem to indicate that masturbation is being described.

The woman's way of killing herself obviously symbolizes oral
intercourse. She takes a revolver and heats it in water, so that "the
barrel would acquire human temperature for the anxious mouth"
(p. 164). Onetti's description of her feelings as the bullet enters
her brain is explicit: ". . . she thought that she again had spilled
in her mouth the taste of the man, so similar to fresh grass, to
happiness, and to summer" (pp. 164–165).

This is the clearest symbolic image in the entire story, and two
immediate questions arise from the action: What is its meaning
in relation to the personality of the woman? and Why has she
given it such importance as the last act of her life? There are no
definite answers commensurate with the clarity of the symbolic
meaning.

There are, again, several possibilities. The first is that the woman's suicide is an act of surrender to masculinity and a destruction of the feminine self, made more complete by the perverted
nature of the action. This interpretation is supported by the
symbolic context of the story and the male-female polarity that
develops from this symbolism. The other possibility is that the
form of the action indicates only partial surrender to heterosexual drives. The essence of the woman's femininity does not
participate.

The last paragraph of the novel recounts almost exactly the
dream at the beginning of the novel. Again this repetition gives
an impression of clarity and completeness that masks the ambiguity of meaning of the image. Among the differences between
the two dreams is one that is important because it symbolically
indicates what has taken place in the novel. In the first dream the
woman is described as "carrying an empty suitcase" (p. 137).
This seems to be a symbol for a deficient feminine sexuality. At
the end of the novel the description is different. The woman is
"twisted by the suitcase" (p. 165), deformed by her sexuality. As

has been seen, this deformation is the major cause of her suicide.

Thus, the woman's alienation and loss of self, like Eladio Linacero's, are due to personal factors, the foremost of which is a defective sexuality. The woman's being is polarized or split, and heterosexuality becomes destructive. Her fear of masculinity is so great that she is unable to feel anything but hate for her son. She needs love but can attain only promiscuity.

Her life is presented through a series of symbols with a common feature, ambiguity. In most cases the images show surface coherence with increasing fragmentation as deeper levels of meaning are sought. Several images seem to reverse the process; they show surface fragmentation and lack of meaning but have significance at depth. The result is the same as that of the techniques of imagery in *El pozo*: a quantitative and qualitative reproduction of a schizophrenic world, but a world much more extensive than that in *El pozo*.

In addition, a few of the author's fundamental attitudes are visible in *Tan triste como ella*. The most revealing is a belief in the destructive force of life, in the inevitable unhappiness caused by living. Other attitudes may be inferred from the themes common to *Tan triste* and *El pozo*. The loss of innocence that comes with sexual awakening, with resultant unhappiness, is the clearest of these.

One further question must be asked before the discussion of *Tan triste* is ended. In Onetti's world of desperate people firmly rooted in their belief in the essential horror of life, why do so few of them commit suicide? There are only four important characters in all his works who kill themselves. A few others allow themselves to die. But of the four suicides—Elena Salas in *La vida breve*, the woman in *Tan triste*, Julita in *Juntacadáveres*, Risso in "El infierno tan temido"—three are women. The only thing these figures have in common is their failure to avoid unacceptable reality through evasive activity. Elena Salas and the woman in *Tan triste* make no attempt at evasion and thus cannot tolerate life. Julita evades through insanity, but when this evasion no longer serves she kills herself. Risso is forced by a woman into a

situation in which he has no power to evade. At the other end of
the spectrum, Larsen, the man who endures, does so because he is
an artist of evasion. Thus evasion per se in Onetti's novels becomes a life-giving force. The reflection of this attitude in his
artistic techniques has already been seen in the evasion, or deceit,
of the narrator in *El pozo* and in the equivocal statements that
can be attributed to the author in *Tan triste*. However, the most
characteristic form of evasion seen in all Onetti's works is the
ambiguity surrounding all actions, images, and attitudes. In the
sense that this ambiguity separates the author from his work, the
reader from the content, and the characters from themselves, it
is another form of alienation.

No discussion of this subject would be complete without men-
tion of two other works, *La vida breve* and *El astillero*, which
show several aspects of alienation not seen in the two short novels
already studied. The most important aspect is social alienation.
The other is the relation of action to the alienated man. Only
these two subjects will be discussed to any extent and no detailed
analysis of the two works will be attempted.

An initial similarity exists between Brausen, the protagonist of
La vida breve, and Eladio Linacero. Both men project their lives
into imaginary structures, the marriages of both have failed for
the same reasons that all marriages fail in Onetti's creations. Beyond these points of similarity resemblance diminishes. Brausen
is a much more intelligent and complex person than Linacero. He
is highly articulate and, more importantly, shows a great deal of
self-knowledge. The greatest difference between him and Linacero is that he is a man in society and is both conscious and critical of that society on an intellectual level, free from his personal
necessities. In addition he is capable of action.

The clarity of Brausen's self-definitions and his frequent discussions of the meaning of his creation of other lives make the
conditions of his alienation clear. His first definition locates him
in terms of personal history and of society. "Meanwhile, I am this
small and timid man, unchangeable, married to the only woman
I seduced, or who seduced me, incapable not only of being an-

other but even of the will to be another. The little man who disgusts as much as he causes pity, a small man lost in the legion of
small men who were promised the Kingdom of Heaven. This one,
me in the taxicab, inexistent, the mere incarnation of the idea of
Juan María Brausen, a biped symbol of a cheap puritanism made
of negatives."[23] His alienation is measured by the distance he is
separated from himself in order to have the perspective to make
this description. It is also seen in his self-disgust. Further, emotional alienation is seen in his opinion of his own morality. It is
also shown in his relation to his wife: he is separated from her to
the point that he does not know the emotional nature of a pivotal
action in their lives.

The social alienation expressed in the lines quoted is of interest
because it is not evident in the two works discussed previously. In
one way it is similar to the limited view of society seen in *El pozo*;
Brausen, like Linacero, is projecting his concept of himself onto
other people. The new element is the concept of mass man. Brausen sees himself as lost and faceless in surrounding humanity.
This feature of alienation is important in the descriptions of the
subject by all modern commentators, who believe that man loses
his identity among large numbers of his fellow beings.

Marx based his definition of alienation on the human conditions created by industrial labor that allowed the worker no vital
contact with the product of his work. This aspect of alienation is
present in *La vida breve*. Brausen knows that work is one of the
factors of his unhappiness. "Gertrudis and filthy work and the
fear of losing it—I was thinking, arm and arm with Stein—the
bills to be paid and the unforgettable surety that nowhere is there
a woman, a friend, a house, a book, not even a vice that can make
me happy" (p. 52). His objection to his work is in terms of general human values, whereas in his earlier description of mass man
his self-disgust determined his reaction.

I returned at nightfall to the agency to deliver reports and to explain
with patience and humility how I had spent the day, without letting
down my vigilance over the firm tone of voice with which I developed

promises of future accounts, anticipated satisfactory transactions, explained how and why the negatives of today would become tomorrow's contracts; I spoke caressing my moustache, lifting it so that my lip would show a smile of communicable confidence, without ceasing to listen to the voices, the rings, and the noises of doors, trying not to be taken by surprise by the invitation to "drop by the office of Mr. Macleod, Mr. Macleod would like you to do so, before you leave," the first sentence of the touching, protective, and lying series with which the old man would let me know that I was fired. (P. 72)

Brausen's alienation here is due to his being forced to play a part he despises and that is self-destructive. In addition, he has no control over the results of his actions; they are something separate from him that arises in response to the fear of losing his job.

Brausen's direct and indirect criticism is only a part of his social vision. He is specific in his condemnation of the artificiality of modern consumer society. "He caught a taxi at the corner and I saw the last wave of his hand, I saw him go away, in the beginning of the night, toward the poetic, musical, and plastic world of tomorrow, toward our common destiny of more automobiles, more toothpaste, more laxatives, more napkins, more refrigerators, more clocks, more radios, toward the pallid silent frenzy of the worm's nest" (p. 153).

Thus a large part of Brausen's alienation is due to the form of his society, and he recognizes this fact. He also sees social aspects in the deeper levels of loss of self. "Because each one accepts what he keeps discovering about himself in the looks of others, one is formed from living with others, and blends with what others suppose him to be, and acts according to what is expected from this inexistent being" (p. 239). Brausen rejects this way of creation of self. Instead, he destroys the self that is associated with the life of Juan María Brausen. By separating from his wife, by being fired from his job, by ceasing to associate with his companions, and by isolating himself in his room, he eliminates his social and emotional self and attempts to construct other imaginary selves, believing that he retains that which is essential to his existence. "And one is only condemned to a soul, to a way of

being. One can live many times, many more or less long lives"
(p. 173). It is in the creation of multiple lives other than his own
that Brausen finds his own feeling of life. "And I began to live
again, separated from the everyday deaths, from the bustle and
the crowd in the streets, from the interviews and the never-domi-
nated professional cordiality, I felt a little bit of red hair grow,
like a lung, inside my head, I looked through the spectacles and
the windowpanes of the clinic in Santa María . . ." (p. 131). The
world he creates around Santa María and Díaz Grey is entirely
imaginary and acquires life only through its extension and con-
sistency. Díaz Grey's reality is established when he becomes
aware of his creator, referring to him as "my Brausen." Brausen
participates in his other creation, Arce, to the point that he entirely eradicates his own self. In doing so he repeats a pattern
seen in *El pozo*. He and Linacero fail in marriage for essentially
the same reasons, which are also seen in *Tan triste*. They both,
after several other attempts, establish contact with prostitutes, a
clear affirmation of loss of self. The prostitute by definition is
the woman with whom intimacy leading to surrender of self is
impossible.

Despite literary complications in the form of a novel within a
novel, the psychological base of Brausen's imaginary world is
schizoid. In the works already discussed, schizoid fragmentation
of visual and emotional patterns is evident. In *La vida breve* the
author is trying to produce the totality of the schizoid experience.
R. D. Laing's definition, already quoted in reference to Bombal,
fits Brausen: "The term schizoid refers to an individual the totality of whose experience is split in two main ways: in the first
place, there is a rent in his relation with his world and, in the
second, there is a disruption of his relation with himself . . . he
experiences himself in despairing aloneness and isolation; more-
over, he does not experience himself as a complete person but
rather as 'split' in various ways, perhaps as a mind more or less
tenuously linked to a body, as two or more selves, and so on."[24]
However, the book is not concerned with and does not encourage
an external judgment of Brausen. Brausen's motives, attitudes,

and lives, as created within the work, form the only perspective
of the novel.

Brausen makes several statements about the importance of his
other lives. Worth further discussion is his already quoted statement that a person "is only condemned to a soul, to a way of
being. One can live many times, many more or less long lives."
Onetti in no way defines what he means by "soul" or "way of
being." The wording appears to eliminate the existential position
of Sartre that existence precedes essence. Onetti seems rather to
be talking about essence and form. However, the wording could
be interpreted to refer to both existence and essence. The ambiguity of the quotation is its only certain feature.

Brausen refers to another aspect of his creation of other lives
when he says, "with the certainty of death conquered by my
triple prolongation in time" (p. 188). Superficially this quotation
seems more logical than the previous one. However, if, as the
statement indicates, he considers himself to be three people,
Brausen, Arce, and Díaz Grey, then what is the meaning of "my
death"? He cannot be referring to physical death, because all the
lives will end with that. The only meaning that a closer examination can attach to the statement is one connected with loss of self.
If he believes that by splitting his self into three parts he has
avoided the death inherent in the condition of man with a unique
self, then the quotation makes sense. But the process it defines is
the destruction of self in order to avoid the death of self that is
part of living.

Brausen's final statement when he is arrested with Ernesto
adds to the understanding of his motives. "This was what I had
been searching for since the beginning, since the death of the
man who lived five years with Gertrudis: to be free, to be irre-
sponsible in the presence of others, to conquer myself without
effort in true solitude" (p. 276). The solitude desired is that resulting from total alienation and from complete destruction of
self. The self he desires to conquer is that which, free from all
external human contacts and actions, is the minimum definition
of an individual existence. It would seem that Brausen's goal is

self-destruction, covered by a false desire for self-definition. If
self-definition, definition of the essential self, were his true
motive, then some indication would be present, either in actions
or in attitudes, as to what the self would be. Instead only absolute solitude and self-destruction are evident.

It is Onetti who gives the novel a final ambiguous direction.
Brausen disappears and the book ends with an adventure with
Díaz Grey, who now has a life and personality of his own. He is
no longer dependent on Brausen the creator. The ambiguity
arises in the relation of Díaz Grey's autonomy to Brausen's conquest of self. No evidence is available to indicate the nature of
the relation. The only certainty is that Onetti, as author-creator,
has taken the place of Brausen, the creator of other lives.

It is hoped that this brief discussion of *La vida breve* has
shown that there are two separate influences in it leading to
alienation and loss of self. Onetti, through Brausen, makes a specific criticism of modern society and the conditions of impersonal
labor, showing their destructive force on the personality. The
other influence leading to alienation and destruction of self is the
psychology of the character. The terms of this psychology are
essentially the same as those seen in the other works studied:
disgust with life, failure of marriage, desire for self-destruction.
The world that Brausen creates while in the process of destruction of self was seen to be schizoid in form.

Larsen, the protagonist of *El astillero*, is the opposite of Brausen, in that his life is concerned with the maintenance of self in
the face of a hostile and overwhelming world. Díaz Grey describes the heroic side of Larsen's existence, calling Larsen "this
man who lived the last thirty years on filthy money given him
with pleasure by filthy women; who hit upon defending himself
against life by substituting for it a treachery without origin; this
man of toughness and courage, who used to think in one fashion
and now thinks in another; who wasn't born to die but instead to
win and impose himself; who at this moment is imagining life as
an infinite and timeless territory in which it is necessary to ad-
vance and to take advantage."[25] This heroic quality does not

mean that Larsen is not alienated, because he is, but to a much
lesser degree than Brausen. He maintains a functional self in the
face of his alienation and failure.

As in *La vida breve*, there is an important social element in *El
astillero*, indicated by the title. The relation between Larsen and
the dead shipyard is the central feature of the novel. Larsen's
entire personality is revealed in his attitudes and activities with
respect to the shipyard. His relation to his job is much more complex than that of Brausen to his job in *La vida breve*. To begin
with, he knows the job is meaningless, but he converts it into a
defense against life. "Aside from the farce that he had literally
accepted as an employment, there were only winter, old age,
having nowhere to go, the same possibility of death" (p. 77).
Brausen, alienated by his work, flees from it. Larsen accepts the
alienation and manipulates it, "needing to believe that all was his
and needing to completely deliver himself to it, with the only
aim of giving him a meaning and attributing this meaning to his
remaining years" (p. 37). The result of Larsen's efforts is the
conversion of the shipyard into a separate world. He recognizes
what has happened but is not worried by it.

The most important difference between Larsen and Brausen
is that the former can act both in the real world and in the one
ordered by his imagination, and the latter only in his created
world. In addition Larsen can function with full knowledge of his
alienation from all that surrounds him, believing in the complete
meaninglessness of his actions.

A newly born sun was trying out its apathetic rays of clarity. "Morning, a beautiful fresh winter morning," he thought, in order to with-
draw. Afterward, because there is no courage without forgetfulness:
"This winter's light in a day without wind and fixed in it, while it,
disinterested and cold, is surrounding me and looking at me. I will
do, just because, as indifferent as the white radiance that is shining
on me, acts number one, number two, and number three, and so on
until I have to stop, because of conformity or weariness, admitting that
something incomprehensible, perhaps useful for someone, has been
accomplished by my mediation." (P. 107)

Thus by action he can uphold a minimal self in a meaningless world.

When Larsen is faced by total failure, without future, alienated from his body and his external existence, he still maintains a self that gives him the will to act in the face of meaninglessness. "He was alone, definitively and without drama. He strode along, slowly, without will and without urgency, without the possibility or desire of choice, through a territory whose map was shrinking hour by hour. He had the problem—not him: his bones, his sinews, his shadow—of arriving on time at an unknown and exact place and instant; he had—from no one—the promise that the date would be kept" (p. 178). The narrator, of uncertain identity, judges Larsen's existence at this point—"Thus nothing more than a man, this one, Larsen . . ." (p. 178)—indicating Larsen's reduction to his essential self.

Onetti does not allow Larsen's posture to remain unequivocal to the end. Two possible endings are given, the origins of which are unknown to the reader. In one Larsen leaves, defeated but intact. In the other he is destroyed—humiliated by the boatmen, incoherent; he dies shortly thereafter. The reader must choose. The ambiguity of the ending vitiates any generalization about the positive values represented by Larsen, as it is not certain to what extent he maintains them in the face of his failure. Thus any retrospective judgment of these positive values must be relative to their position in the novel and to their possible final collapse.

There is another area of ambiguity touched upon that should be mentioned before this discussion of El astillero is ended. This area concerns the narration itself or, more exactly, the point of view and identity of the narrator. The use of the first person plural relates him to the town of Santa María, as does his interest in events pertaining to the town. The scenes presented, on the other hand, make him omniscient. This omniscience in turn is confused by the equivocal nature of the ending. A similar confusion of narrative planes takes place in Juntacadáveres, but it is difficult to say what its effect is because of the intermingling of other lives and their impingement on Larsen. One must suspect a deliberate attempt to cloud any positive interpretation of Larsen.

Nevertheless, what does emerge from *El astillero* is a pattern of alienation that does not seem to lead to loss of self. The will to act, although the actions be meaningless, preserves and defines the essential self. Because of this will to act the alienating conditions of society and life may be met and held at bay.

4. Alejo Carpentier: Alienation, Culture, and Myth

Alejo Carpentier's first novel, *Ecue-Yamba-O*, was written in 1927 and published in 1933.[1] The novel was an attempt to describe Afro-Cuban culture. A trip to Haiti in 1943 provided material for his second novel, *El reino de este mundo*, which was not published until 1949. His story "Viaje a la semilla," in an edition limited to one hundred copies, was printed in 1944. After several years of work his book *La música en Cuba* was published in 1946. A journey to the upper Orinoco in 1947 gave him the idea for *Los pasos perdidos*, which was published in 1953. *El acoso*, a short novel, appeared in 1956. Between 1956 and 1959 he worked on his other major novel, *El siglo de las luces*.

During his early years in Cuba, Carpentier was part of the vanguardist movement. "These affirmations of Carpentier permit us to firmly establish that the essential feature of the years 1920–1928 is that the author fully participates in Cuban vanguardism, sharing the desires of his countrymen and finding friends and collaborators among the principal figures of the group."[2] His first novel, *Ecue-Yamba-O*, was written during this period but reworked after he went to Paris, where he came in contact with the surrealist movement. He met all the major figures of this movement and published several surrealist stories, but drew away from the movement when he felt he could add nothing new to it. His major interest was in the expression of the essence of the Latin American world. *Los pasos perdidos* is the full realization of his efforts in this direction.

Carpentier, in *Tientos y diferencias*, defines his concept of what the Latin American novel should be. Two aspects of it are central to any discussion of his writing. The first, and the dominant note in his work, is "marvelous reality," which he sees as the essence of Latin American reality. Angel Flores, using the term "magical realism" and extending the concept to cover a number of contemporary writers, defines it as a fusion of the real and the fantastic.[3] Carlos Santander in his excellent article "Lo maravilloso en la obra de Alejo Carpentier" gives a more precise and functional definition of the "marvelous" modification of the real: "... the concept of 'the marvelous' will consist of a 'second reality' that operates from astonishment, capable of stimulating the imagination and of awakening a willful attitude."[4] For a character to perceive reality modified in such a fashion would be the opposite of alienated perception. In *Los pasos perdidos* the movement by the narrator from complete alienation toward experiencing this special reality allows the study of the full process of alienation. In the works of the other authors examined in this study there has been no contrast within a character between alienated and unalienated states. The movement has been from lesser to greater alienation or the reverse.

The second aspect of importance in Carpentier's concept of the Latin American novel is his idea of the correct form necessary to express a unique Latin American reality. He considers a baroque style the only one adequate. His concept of the baroque centers in the manner of description of objects. "But it turns out that now we, the Latin American novelists, have to name everything, everything that defines us, that surrounds and encircles us: everything that operates with an energy of context—in order to place it in the universal."[5] The prose that will give the named objects life "is a baroque prose, of necessity baroque, as is all prose that encircles detail, that describes it fully, coloring it, making it stand out in order to emphasize it and to define it."[6] A perception of objects that has the goal of making them live is a nonalienated perception. As will be seen, in *Los pasos perdidos* the protagonist moves away from the alienation he felt in a northern city when he returns to Latin America and begins to relate to objects and sensations that formed part of his forgotten childhood.

Although Carpentier has declared his intention to name and describe as much as possible of that which is genuinely American, he does not extend this aesthetic to all levels of narration in *Los pasos perdidos*. As Carlos Santander says: ". . . in the text itself there is an absolute omission of any geographic precision. The intelligible stratum—action, personalities, environment—acquires, when this recourse is complemented with others, the value of a metaphoric countryside with permanent symbolic connotations."[7] The direction taken by the symbolism is toward the creation of myth, as noted by Julieta Campos in a brief discussion of *Los pasos perdidos*. "Once more Carpentier shows us the world through myth; he puts imagination to work in order to discover that most profound reality latent beneath the most obvious reality."[8] Thus the relation of alienation to myth, as presented in the novel, will be of interest as a new aspect of the subject not seen in the other authors studied.

Alienation is a major theme in *Los pasos perdidos*. In a conversation with César Leante, quoted by Carlos Santander, Carpentier describes one aspect of the protagonist's alienation during the voyage up the river. "My character in *Los pasos perdidos* travels along it to the roots of life, but when he wants to rediscover life he no longer can, since he has lost access to his authentic existence. This is the thesis of the novel, which cost me no little effort in writing."[9] In a conversation with Salvador Bueno, Carpentier presents another feature of the theme. "An idea dominates *Los pasos perdidos*: that of a possible evasion in time."[10] Thus alienation in time becomes an additional dimension to be examined.

Another aspect of alienation of importance in the novel has not received much attention from critics, yet it stands at the center of the narrator's journey through time. This aspect is cultural alienation. A cultural time is the substance of the protagonist's journey. He makes contact with and reacts to three different cultures and to several subcultures within them. His discovery of the marvelous comes about through his contact with a primitive society. Cultural factors influence his final assessment of his condition: a series of new perspectives gained by his reexamination of what he thought his original relation to the primitive culture was, due in turn to the contrast between the primitive culture and his reentry into modern Western society.

The alienation in *Los pasos perdidos* will be studied in connection with the stages in the narrator's journey. This procedure is almost mandatory because these stages represent an emotional, symbolic, and mythic progression from one state to another. In addition, the structure of the book coincides with that of the journey. Special attention will be paid to the difference between the protagonist's reactions to modern society before and after his journey. No attempt will be made to fully trace the development of symbolism in the novel. This task has been done thoroughly by Carlos Santander, Klaus Müller-Bergh, Juan Loveluck, and others, and these critics will be referred to when appropriate. Only the features of symbolism and myth that are important to the theme of alienation will be discussed.

Three aspects of the protagonist's life in the city are central to the understanding of his alienation at the beginning of the novel. They are his work, his relation to his wife and to his mistress, and his reaction to the society of the city. The first of these, his work, must further be divided into his concept of work in society and the personal problem of art and work.

The first feature of work discussed at length by the narrator is the destructive force of repetitive meaningless actions: ". . . my wife let herself be carried along by the automatism of imposed work, as I let myself be carried by the automatism of my occupation."[11] He explores the effects of this automatism on himself,

his wife, their marriage, and man in general. It leads him to flight
from himself. "Bound to my technique amid clocks, chrono-
graphs, metronomes, in windowless rooms with carpets and
soundproofing, always in an artificial place, I instinctively
· searched for, on finding myself every afternoon on the already
darkened street, pleasures that would make me forget the passage of time. I drank and amused myself until drink and amusement put me to sleep next to an alarm clock . . ." (p. 15). This
quotation emphasizes, in addition to repetition, the artificiality of
environment that is a part of modern work. This is, of course, a
very important theme in *Los pasos perdidos* in the sense that the
journey undertaken by the narrator results in discovery of and
participation in a natural environment. The nature of his participation will be discussed later, but the disgust with artificiality
of surroundings expressed in the lines quoted and the alienation
arising from it are reiterated throughout the description of existence in a modern northern city and must be considered as basic
features of the protagonist's life.

The personal alienation due to this kind of life is clearly seen
by the narrator. "There were great gaps of weeks and weeks in
the record of my own existence; spells of which I hadn't a single
recollection, the trace of an exceptional feeling or of an enduring emotion; days in which I had the obsessive impression that
my every gesture had been made before in identical circumstances . . ." (p. 14).

His wife is also trapped by her job, a part in a play that has
been running for years. The success arising from this part has
obliterated any of her earlier aspirations and left her with only
the repetition of empty gestures. The rhythm imposed on each of
them by their employment keeps them physically apart. He
works during the day and she at night. The repetitive automatism
extends to the essence of married life; they sleep together every
seventh day, making their emotional and physical needs servants
to their work.

Carpentier's use of biblical motifs may give, in retrospect, a
deeper symbolic meaning to sexual union on the seventh day. In

the Bible there are two areas important for their seven-day se-
quences, the book of Genesis, with the seven days of creation,
and Revelations, with the opening of the seven seals. Both are
mentioned in *Los pasos perdidos*. As Carlos Santander has
pointed out, and as the narrator observes, the days of creation are
important as a symbolic background for the stages of the journey.
However, the seventh day is never reached. The seals are mentioned several times in the narrative and are not as integrated into
the structure of the novel as are the days of creation of Genesis.
The context of alienation and failure and the essential nature of
the day together of husband and wife would seem to indicate a
relation to the opening of the seventh seal. However, there is no
firm evidence beyond the emphasis on the number seven to
allow a definite conclusion.

   The alienation presented to this point is that described by
Marx and Fromm, with few modifications. It is shown arising
from conditions of work and from the environment of a modern
city. The result is exactly as described by Erich Fromm: a feeling
of lack of control over one's life and of detachment from the self.
However, Carpentier does not stay within the limits of alienation
due to social and economic factors. His initial departure from
these limits is in the occupation of the narrator and his wife; they
are both artists. This fact makes Marx's concept of alienation less
applicable because of its focus on the laborer and the total lack
of his identification with the product of his labor. The same quali-
fication applies to Fromm's ideas, except that he describes an
alienating society of much greater influence and scope. The artist
will always in some way feel vitally related to his work, because,
no matter what the conditions of its use, it is always a product of
his being. The artist's alienation in respect to his work arises
from the use to which he sees his product put and from his knowledge of the gap between the possibilities of his art, art in general,
and the artistic value of what he creates in response to the re-
quirements imposed on him. Carpentier is aware of this problem
in *Los pasos perdidos* and focuses directly on it when the narrator describes the viewing of a film for which he supplied the

music. The repetition of the film for new arrivals at the party initiates a process of alienation, separating the narrator gradually from his vital connection with his work. When he is sufficiently distanced emotionally from the film, he is able to focus on the cause of his growing alienation from it. "A certainty was poisoning my initial satisfaction: it was that all that fierce work, the displays of good taste, the professional dominance, the selection and coordination of my collaborators and assistants, had given birth, when all was said and done, to a public relations film, commissioned with the firm that employed me by a fishing consortium, joined in ferocious battle with a net of cooperatives" (p. 31). In other words, it is not his lack of relation to the product of his labor that causes alienation, as described by Marx and Fromm; it is the social use to which it is put. An additional, more subtle factor, repetition, also serves to distance him. Meaninglessness as a product of repetition has already been seen to cause alienation, both from his wife and from his job. Now, on a higher level, it separates him from the results of his art, just as it has his wife. She no longer aspires to play the great roles that would be a fulfillment of her life as an artist. This same empty repetition has extended to the sexual act, the core of their married life and, on a more general level, the cornerstone of any permanent male-female alliance. The nonrepetitive yet constant nature of his sexual relation with Rosario later in the novel serves to illustrate by contrast the use of repetition as a technique to reveal the sterility of his relationship with his wife.

However, when the narrator generalizes on man's condition in modern society he reaches the same conclusion as do Marx and Fromm; man has lost his soul to organized industrial society. "We had fallen into the era of the Wasp-Man, of the No-Man, in which souls were not sold to the Devil but, instead, to the Bookkeeper or to the Slave Master" (p. 15). This quotation shows for the first time another feature that will be important throughout the novel. The terms used are generic, but the use of capital letters extends their meaning beyond simple generalizations. *Bookkeeper* and *Slave Master* suggest superhuman qualities. The same technique is applied to an individual, the Curador ("Curator"), who appears in the first part of the novel and who has definite mythic dimensions as a herald of adventure. Also, a wealth of references by the narrator to classical myths in the first few pages creates a mythical orientation in the narrative, reinforcing the connotations of capitalized generic terms.

One other aspect of the narrator's art, music, must be mentioned before discussion of the start of his journey and his steps away from alienation. He interrupts the sequence of events to discuss music. The narrator sees music as an expression of man's—the artist's—will in time. The basic material of the art is the manipulation, division, and measurement of time, and the performance of the work is a monument to the artist's dominance over time and over death itself. Thus the successful completion of the musician's will is a vital, nonalienated action that lifts him beyond the human condition. This action is in direct contrast to the use of art by the protagonist, who is subject to both time and economics. His alienation from his art becomes clearer because of this comparison.

The narrator's journey, his "evasion of epoch," is not initiated by his contact with the Curador, as is thought by most critics. This chance encounter would have had no result, beyond the narrator's realization of his spiritual emptiness, had not the planned pattern of his existence been interrupted by his wife's unexpected departure at the start of his vacation. The aimlessness that results from her leaving sends him into the street and is the occasion of his meeting the Curador. On the level of plot and action the Curador serves to remind the narrator of what he had been and of the unfulfilled promise of his present existence; he also offers the mechanism of escape from the life of alienation accepted by the protagonist. The offered evasion is rejected. The real first step in the narrator's journey is the change from the influence of his wife to that of another woman, his mistress Mouche. She is the one, excited by what she considers to be the possibility of adventure, who makes the decision, against the will of the narrator. He is afraid of the emptiness of his vacation, "waking up with nothing to do, and the fear of meeting a person, taken from myself, who every year waited for me at the start of my vacation" (p. 37). Yet he sees the trip as another form of servitude: ". . . that meeting which provoked a change of burden, since where I dropped Sisyphus's boulder, another was placed on my still-aching shoulder" (p. 37). In the first step, then, the will to action, to adventure, is absent. The protagonist submits to the will of others.

Many critics emphasize the heroic aspects of *Los pasos perdidos*. Juan Loveluck states: "*Los pasos perdidos* is a new venture of Ulysses. There is a long hazardous voyage. The hero-narrator gradually divests himself of false coverings, links, and temptations."[12] As will be seen at each new stage of the journey, however, the narrator lacks any will to heroism or to adventure. In most cases the narrator goes on in reaction to situations, to escape them, rather than from a desire to go forward.

The nature of the search—an effort to encounter musical instruments that support a theory no longer of any vital interest to the narrator—is another feature of nonheroic dimensions. Its result would be of interest to few people and would be restricted to the closed world of the Curador. The general mythic pattern of the hero returning from the voyage with something of great value for mankind would hardly be followed by these initial conditions. Certainly the description by Carpentier of the journey as "an evasion" implies something other than mythical heroism.

This objection does not deny the mythic aspects of the journey. The narration is full of allusions to Ulysses, Prometheus, legendary explorers, and others. Klaus Müller-Bergh has clearly defined the function of mythical references in *Los pasos perdidos*:

Now then, although there are many mythological parallels with Sisyphus, Prometheus, and Ulysses, which we have already noted, they do not furnish, in our view, more than the skeleton of the structure of *Los pasos perdidos*, not the structure itself. These parallels are not substantial elements of the personality of our man. They are no more than erudite allusions, irrelevant in regard to the nature of the character. They reflect, without doubt, the intellectual character of the work, but their principal function is that of helping to organize the narrative material and the theme of the artist in the modern epoch. If the figure of the hero is likeable and probable it is because the protagonist has roots in the Spanish-speaking earth and in the totality of the Hispanic world.[13]

Carlos Santander approaches the mythic dimension of *Los pasos perdidos* from a different direction, applying the ideas of Joseph Campbell's book *The Hero with a Thousand Faces*, a cross-cultural study of the mythic hero from a psychoanalytic standpoint. Campbell uses the term *monomyth* to describe the generic form of the mythological adventure: "A hero adventures forth from the world of common day into a region of supernatural wonder; fabulous forces are there encountered and a decisive victory is won: the hero comes back from this mysterious adventure with the power to bestow boons on his fellow man."[14] Various steps are common to all mythical adventures described. Many of the aspects of the journey in *Los pasos perdidos* correspond with Campbell's description, particularly the transition from a common-day world to one filled with wonder. A major difference is that the marvelous in *Los pasos perdidos* is natural and not supernatural. Also, as will be seen, the protagonist does not return able to "bestow boons on his fellow man." Campbell describes several qualities necessary to heroism that are absent in the narrator. He believes the hero should go beyond his personal limitations to a position of general validity in human and cultural terms. It will be seen that the protagonist in *Los pasos perdidos* does not transcend his limitations. He never transcends his artistic self. Also, Campbell believes the hero should respond to the call to adventure. The lack of response on the part of the main figure in the early part of the narrative has already been outlined, and further examples will be seen.

Another aspect of the antiheroic stance of the narrator is his easy acceptance of Mouche's plan to deceive the Curador and to use money from him for a paid vacation in Latin America. This additional lack of interest can be interpreted, in Campbell's terms, as a further refusal to answer the call of heroic adventure.

The destination of the first step of the trip is a large Latin American city. That the city is in direct contrast to its northern counterpart is obvious. Salvador Bueno has pointed out the importance of counterpoint as a structural element in *Los pasos perdidos*: "A good part of the book is carried out in a contrapuntal manner."[15] Certainly this observation seems true with respect to some of the characters, such as Rosario and Mouche, as shown by Bueno. It is not true of the cities. Although they are contrasted, they form part of a series, the characteristic of which is that each new center of population is smaller and simpler than the preceding one. This characteristic parallels the nature of the journey. The only contrapuntal aspect involved is the juxtaposition of cultures represented by the two cities. The narrator's description is concerned with the differences between the two based on culture and expressed through the discovery of objects.

Thus the alienated man seen in the first chapter begins to shed his alienation. This change is indicated by the quotation from Shelley at the start of the second chapter: "Ha! I scent life!" Aside from a mythical allusion to Prometheus, the reference is clearly to the narrator's movement away from alienation toward a vital realization of life. This realization, in its first stage, occurs through a rediscovery of self due to a renewal of contact with the influences of childhood. The entire second chapter is concerned with rediscovery, of vital contact with elements that had been of great importance to the narrator at an earlier stage in his life.

The first element, one that forms the lens for all subsequent viewing of the Latin American world, is the protagonist's encounter with the language of his youth. "And a force is slowly penetrating me, through my ears and through my pores: the language. Here is, then, the language I spoke in my childhood, the language in which I learned to read and to criticize, the language rusty in my mind from lack of use, put to one side like a useless tool, in a country where it could be of little service to me" (p. 46). The linguistic aspects mentioned of importance to the narrator are those of the formation of an intelligent nonalienated being: the ability to read and, above all, to criticize. Also, with the rediscovery of language the protagonist's relation to his mistress changes. Because of ignorance of the language she must make her contact with the external world through him. He has become the guide, whereas before he had followed her will. The discord between them arises because, while the narrator is extending himself through vital contact and rediscovery, Mouche maintains her same alienated relation to life, which becomes more obvious through her lack of engagement with the new environment. The narrator emphasizes the cultural basis of Mouche's alienation from her surroundings: "I felt irritated, suddenly, by a very habitual selfishness of my friend, that always put her in a position of hostility as soon as she came in contact with something that was ignorant of the passwords of certain artistic surroundings frequented by her in Europe" (p. 50).

The radical nature of Mouche's lack of engagement with her environment and the resulting artificiality of her being become even more evident to the narrator as he begins to renew his contact with the natural world. Overcome with the beauty of the southern constellations, he realizes that Mouche, the astrologer, has no knowledge of the real nature of the stars.

The move to Los Altos increases the distance between them, a distance accompanied by the narrator's growing suspicion concerning Mouche's tendencies toward lesbianism. However, the essential passivity of will seen in the protagonist's lack of decision at the start of the journey is again evident. He and Mouche go to Los Altos because, due to a revolution, life in the city has become unpleasant and the planned holiday is no longer possible. The narrator's first definite act of will is not seen until he decides to leave Los Altos and search for the musical instruments that are the original justification of the trip. The reasons for that decision, their relation to the narrator's movement away from alienation, and the importance they have with respect to the interpretation of the next stage of the journey require careful consideration.

The village of Los Altos itself has an effect on the protagonist. His first reaction to it is of interest. "Nothing that could be seen

was monumental or renowned; nothing had yet gotten on a post-
card, nor was it praised in guidebooks. Yet, nevertheless, in this
provincial backwater, where every corner, every iron-studded
door responded to a particular way of life, I found a delight that,
in the museum towns, had been lost by the too-manipulated and
too-photographed stones" (p. 70). This is a further rediscovery
of the nonalienated life of his youth, the visual forms of which
reflect its harmony. The narrator is aware of the changes in himself brought about by his environment and of the fact that it is
separating him from Mouche. "While the changes of altitude, the
cleanness of the air, the upheaval of habits, the reencounter with
the language of my childhood, were causing in me a kind of regression, still vacillating but perceptible, to an equilibrium lost
long ago, in her could be seen, although she would not yet admit
it, signs of boredom. Nothing of what we had already seen cor-
responded, evidently, to what she had hoped to find on this trip,
if she had hoped to find anything, really" (p. 73).

However, the real importance of the brief stay in Los Altos is
that the two major themes of the novel—art and nature—come
together for the first time. The theme of nature, in the form of
the narrator's encounter with it in its most primitive state, is
going to occupy the largest remaining part of the novel, and Los
Altos is the point of departure. The two themes meet when three
artists come to the house where the narrator and Mouche are
staying. They are almost completely symbolic figures. The narrator associates them with the Magi, but they also are, because
they represent the three races of South America, symbolic of the
art that should arise from the fusion of these races. However, as
artists they are alienated from their heritage, interested only in
European forms and totally ignorant of the reality and unique-
ness of their environment. Carpentier, through the narrator, puts
them in relation to nature. "I asked them then, to keep my friend
from talking, if they had been toward the jungle. The Indian poet
answered, shrugging his shoulders, that there was nothing to be
seen in that direction . . ." (p. 76). The narrator's judgment of
their vitality is also related to Latin American nature. "I saw

them becoming weak and pale in their studies without light, the Indian olivaceous, the Negro without smiles, the white soured, always more forgetful of the Sun left behind" (p. 77). They provide him with insight concerning his own loss of authenticity. However, this new level of self-knowledge has behind it the weight of all the rediscoveries he had made since returning to Latin America. The insight is both personal and artistic. "I perceived this night, looking at them, how much damage had been done me by early uprooting from this environment that had been mine until adolescence, how much had been contributed to my loss of orientation by the easy brilliance of the men of my generation, carried away by theories to the same intellectual labyrinths, to be eaten by the same minotaurs" (p. 77). This is the first time the reader is able to begin to form any concept of the "authentic existence" mentioned by Carpentier in his discussion with Salvador Bueno, and it is obvious because of the context that it is related to an awareness of nature in its unique Latin American form.

The result of his meeting the three artists is a new orientation for the narrator toward nature, the consequences of which he does not see. "I would have liked to silence the voices at my back in order to find the diapason of the frogs, the sharp tonality of the cricket . . ." (p. 78). As shown by the manner of description, it is the artistic self of the narrator that becomes responsive to the physical environment. This new orientation does not come to the fore in his decision to leave Los Altos. It remains in the background, visible only as a sensitivity to be incidentally fulfilled by the new stage in the journey. In the foreground are his growing irritation with Mouche and his dislike of the situation at Los Altos. "I was informed that here, too, for several days curfew would be observed at sunset. The disagreeable certainty that our—for me undesirable—intimacy with the Canadian woman would become even more close suddenly turned into a decision that culminated an entire process of reflections and recapitulations. From Los Altos itself the buses left for the port from which, by river, there was a way to reach the great Southern Jungle. We would not go on living the swindle thought up by my friend, since circumstances opposed it at every step along the way" (p. 79). Although this is the first exercise of will by the narrator, it is basically unheroic, a reaction to circumstances, rather than motivated by a call to adventure. The narrator himself doubts his resolve and buys bus tickets to keep from backing out.

The nature of the journey changes when the narrator leaves Los Altos. At the moment of departure the narrator has shed the alienation caused by his form of life in modern society. He has rediscovered and stands in vital relation to the culture, language, and objects of the life of his youth. He is conscious of being an integral person, related to his surroundings. The direct result of this loss of alienation is his ability to exercise his will. "Until now, the move from the capital to Los Altos had been, for me, a kind of regression to the years of my childhood—a going back to adolescence and its beginnings—through the reencounter with ways of life, tastes, words, things that had marked me more deeply than I would have believed" (p. 83). In terms of Carpentier's description of the novel as a journey through time, the first part has been a journey through personal time, which allowed a reestablishment of contact with the narrator's self and a feeling of control over his actions.

Leaving Los Altos, the narrator recognizes the change in the nature of his voyage: "Leaving the opalescent mist that was growing green with dawn would initiate, for me, a sort of Discovery" (p. 84). The description is symbolic in that the dawn of the day corresponds to the dawn of the narrator's new consciousness and his escape from the fog of alienation. At last he is surrounded by nature without the interference of modern Western culture.

Carpentier uses contrast to emphasize the change in the protagonist; as he reacts to the new environment, Mouche becomes more and more alienated from it. "Mouche, on the other hand, was turning out to be tremendously outlandish within a growing maladjustment between herself and everything that surrounded us. An aura of exoticism thickened around her, establishing distances between her figure and all other figures, between her actions, her mannerisms, and the ways of acting that here were normal. She was little by little turning into something strange, out of place, eccentric, that attracted attention . . ." (p. 112). Compared with Mouche is Rosario, a woman who gets on the bus in the mountains: "From morning to afternoon and from afternoon to night she was becoming more authentic, more true, more perfectly outlined in a countryside that became more fixed in character as we approached the river" (p. 113). This is a repetition of a pattern seen at the start of the journey, which began with a change of women. In the next stage, the penetration of the jungle, the narrator travels with Rosario. Mouche returns to civilization, physically defeated by nature. The claim that Carpentier consciously marks the different stages of the journey by changes of women is further supported by the fact that it is immediately after the narrator angrily tells Mouche what his feelings toward her are, when their break becomes open, that he meets the "Commissioner"—the man who has founded a city in the jungle where the protagonist will find what he believes to be complete fulfillment.

The essential passivity of the narrator's nature, seen before, becomes evident again in the last stages of his relation to Mouche. Although he is fully conscious of his dislike of her, the discovery of her infidelity serves only to make him feel more distant and does not initiate any action that would lead to a rupture in their relationship. It is chance, in the form of illness, that causes the separation, not an act of will. He makes love to Rosario only when Mouche collapses from malaria.

The return to civilization represents another change of women, a return to the influence of his wife. Carlos Santander, ignoring the sequential nature of the relationships with women, has picked two women as corresponding to elements in Campbell's description of the monomyth: Rosario, representing the mythic hero's encounter with the goddess, and Ruth, the wife, representing woman as the temptress. Because of the rigid nature of the sequence of women and its relation to the different stages of the journey, the mythic element does not appear to be the object of the narrator's relationships with women. Carpentier seems rather to be presenting a progressive archetypical simplification of the male-female relation that culminates when the narrator and Rosario form "the Pair."

The narrator also describes the process of simplification of human relations in terms of archetypes. "As in the most classical plays the characters were, in this great present and real scene, made of one piece, of Good and Evil: the Perfect Wife, or the Faithful Lover, the Villain and the True Friend, the Mother, worthy or unworthy" (p. 155). These are the forms he sees after he has begun the trip up the river, after Mouche has left. However, he is exposed to the same process of simplification on a cultural level before he arrives at the river, while still on the bus. The first stage is the discovery of a culture centered around the horse, an earlier style of life that the narrator sees as simplifying and enhancing man's existence. "In the Lands of the Horse it seemed that man was more manly. He again was master of millennial techniques that put his hands in direct contact with iron and hide" (p. 120). This quotation is especially important because it marks a change in perspective that the narrator is unaware of until the end of the novel. He has become the observer and does not stand in vital relation to the forms described. His identification with them is internal and emotional. His participation, on the personal level, is with people who have cultural links with him, however tenuous. The Indians always remain completely separate and are described from a great distance.

The next step toward the primitive is the arrival at Puerto Anunciación, a passage from "the Lands of the Horse" to "the Lands of the Dog," from a herding to a hunting culture. "The Dog . . . had maintained, through time, the terms of his original alliance with Man" (p. 126). It is this coexistence of cultures that forms the basis of Carpentier's idea of a journey through time. Only in Latin America does he see the coincidence of different cultural forms that represent different time stages in man's development. The narrator's sense of a journey through time is thus

due to the simultaneous observation of different forms corresponding to different epochs in man's history. He is first aware of
a complete change in his perception of time when he participates
in a form, a mass, that he sees as being exactly the same as that
followed by the conquistadors. "But suddenly I was dazzled by
the revelation that there is no difference between this mass and
the masses of the Conquistadors of the Dorado of long ago. Time
had gone back four centuries" (p. 183). It is his participation—
in the present—in a form from the past that gives him the feeling of a reversal of time. The special feature of this perception is
that it shows an unalienated relation to time and to history.

In the final stages of the journey several events serve to remove
the last traces of the protagonist's alienation. As was shown, Rosario has reduced his relationship to women to the most basic
level. With the formation of "the Pair" all elements that do not
lead to satisfaction between man and woman have been elimi-
nated. Mutual sexual fulfillment is at the center of the new relationship, in direct contrast to the narrator's life with his wife.
In retrospect Mouche is seen to be a step toward complete sexuality, which is made impossible because of her alienation from
her surroundings. Thus what initially appeared as contrast, or, in
Salvador Bueno's terms, counterpoint, is actually a progression
toward simplification.

In terms of alienation Rosario has allowed the narrator to
establish a feeling of intimate contact with his own body. "Never
had I felt so light, so well placed in my body as this morning"
(p. 159).

In addition the protagonist has completed the task he was sent
to do. The result is a new feeling of personal worth. "The re-
demption of the resounding jug—a magnificent piece—was the
first exceptional, memorable act recorded to date in my existence.
The object was growing in my own estimation, tied to my destiny,
abolishing, at that instant, the distance that separated me from
the man who had confided the task to me . . ." (p. 181).

Most important in the narrator's consideration is that he has
passed through several experiences that he describes in terms of

epic trials. The first one, in which Carpentier employs the technique of capitalization he uses so often when he wishes to create mythic or generic connotations, is the trip through a dark threatening passage in the jungle. Nature becomes hostile, menacing. The narrator is made aware of its more terrible aspects of death, decay, and indifference during the passage through the narrow waterway. When it is over he feels as though he has successfully passed through a trial. "When the light came again, I understood that I had passed the First Trial. The shadows had carried away the eve's fear" (p. 170). His heightened perception of primordial beauty he believes to be a result of being tested. The second trial is more violent, a night run down a rain-swollen river where a mistake would mean death. He succumbs to terror. "All reason gone, unable to control my fear, I embrace Rosario, searching for the warmth of her body, not as a lover, but as a child . . ." (p. 176). The already mentioned mass, "the mass of the Conquistadors," is to give thanks for delivery from the river.

These trials share a common feature. Although they are presented with epic overtones, the true position of the narrator is not heroic. His stance is passive. It is his companions who physically confront the danger and overcome it. They participate in that they manage the boats and have knowledge to find their way, and the narrator goes forward because of their efforts. The mere fact of his survival allows him to feel that he has passed the second test: ". . . on knowing that I am again on firm ground, to which Fray Pedro leaped with a 'Praised be the Lord!' I understand that I have passed through the Second Trial" (p. 177). Thus, despite the epic connotations attached to the events, their true significance is internal, in the emotions experienced by the narrator. His relation to the events is really antiheroic: he does nothing and is overcome by fear.

Javier Martínez-Palacio, in his article "Los anti-héroes de Alejo Carpentier," states, "Carpentier, in my opinion, never has believed in the existence of historical heroes."[16] He believes that Carpentier has a definite purpose behind his overall antiheroic attitude; he is attempting to show "the flow of moral instability

that always has characterized the Latin American man."[17] It is
certainly true that one of the outstanding characteristics of the
narrator, before and after his journey, is his moral instability.
Deceit is acceptable to him in the original plans for the trip,
while he is in Santa Mónica, where he does not tell Rosario about
his wife, even though he has decided to tell no lies, and immediately on his return, when he decides to write a false story for a
newspaper. There is one indication of Carpentier's attitude toward the problem. In the first part of the novel the narrator men-
tions the impossibility of heroism in modern society, with its endless repetition of meaningless tasks or events: "But to evade this
repetition, in the world destiny had given me, was as impossible
as trying to relive, in these times, certain gestures of heroism or
sainthood" (p. 15). Of the figures encountered by the narrator,
only one—Fray Pedro—would seem to have heroic qualities. He
is the only person whose will to put his ideals into action results
in a conscious approach to death.

But whatever interpretation is attached to the antiheroic bias,
its existence definitely is antithetical to the presence of any en-
compassing mythical qualities. This bias adds further support to
Klaus Müller-Bergh's description of the secondary function of
mythical elements in *Los pasos perdidos*. He believes that they
are not of primary importance in the formation of the character
of the protagonist and that their major function is structural.[18]

Thus, before arriving at Santa Mónica de los Venados, the narrator has shed all the alienation that characterized him and his reaction to modern society. Yet, before he arrives, there is one more
discovery awaiting him. It is quite important in that it indicates
which theme will be uppermost during his stay at Santa Mónica.
He had thought that the acquisition of the primitive musical instruments had proven his theory of the origin of music, that it
started from an imitation of natural sounds. In an Indian village
he watches a witch doctor attempting to bring a man back to life.
"In the face of Death's obstinacy, that refuses to release its prey,
the Word, suddenly, weakens and becomes disheartened. In the

mouth of the Shaman, the orphic healer, it rattles and falls, con-
vulsively, the Dirge—since this and nothing else is a dirge—leaving me stunned with the revelation that I have just been present
at the Birth of Music" (p. 191). The discovery of the birth of
music leads to the rebirth of his artistic self, and it is the artistic
theme that, in relation to the narrator's essential self, will occupy
the rest of the book. Since it must be considered that the protagonist's evasion of his epoch, according to Carpentier's previously
quoted description, is complete, only his artistic self remains as a
link to what he was. And this artistic self at last comes into full
expression in the form of a will to create. The lack of this desire
was the central element in the narrator's artistic alienation in the
city, where his dissatisfaction came from his using his art in the
market place rather than as a creative, satisfying product.

Santa Mónica also has a structural importance, because it represents the reversal of the process of simplification that began
with the narrator's arrival in Latin America. Once the narrator
renews the practice of his art, his life, starting at the simple level
of need for paper and pencil, becomes subject to new needs. His
relation to Rosario is contaminated by Fray Pedro's scrutiny and
by his own knowledge of his wife in the United States.

When an airplane arrives searching for him, he shows the same
lack of decision seen at the start of the trip. He drinks too much
and can come to no clear conclusion. At last he decides, on the
urging of the pilot, to return, gather the materials he needs to
practice his art, and come back to Santa Mónica to stay. Rosario
does not understand the decision, but this does not worry him. He
leaves the manuscript as a pledge to return.

His experience in the jungle has, of course, changed his reaction to modern society. Some aspects of his nature have not
changed, as has been noted. He is immediately willing to write a
false account of his trip in order to gain money. However, he
faces his wife with the truth, but only when the necessity is forced
on him by her discovery of his relationship with Mouche. Immediately after his break with his wife, he records the sensations

aroused by renewed contact with the city. His perspective is that of the artist looking at the world through the lenses of his medium, in this case rhythm.

As I have acquired the habit of moving to the rhythm of my breathing, I am surprised on discovering that the men around me go, come, cross the wide sidewalk in a rhythm foreign to their organic will. If they walk at a certain pace and not another, it is because their movements correspond to the fixed idea of arriving at the corner in time to see the green light come on, permitting them to cross the avenue. At times the multitude that comes boiling from the trolley doors every so many minutes, with the constancy of a pulsation, seems to break the general rhythm of the street with a more hurried one; but soon the normal time of agitation between signal and signal is reestablished. As I haven't yet succeeded in adjusting to the laws of this movement, I opt for progressing slowly . . . (P. 259)

He is now the observer, maintaining a separate rhythm provided by his experience in the jungle. This position allows him to criticize modern forms, to be separate from them, but, because of the discoveries made in the jungle, without a feeling of alienation. His ideal protects him from the anguish of alienation seen at the beginning and allows him to see the emptiness of modern forms that should be full of human significance. People are "ignorant of the millennial symbolism of their own gestures" (p. 261). Traditions become collective reflexes.

He makes a series of observations before beginning to feel the fear of entrapment for himself. He is able to see the city's sickness even in its buildings: "On my return I find the city covered with ruins more ruined than those accepted as such. Everywhere I see sick columns and agonizing buildings . . ." (p. 261).

He also relates his art to his environment, further idealizing the jungle. "These reflections lead me to believe that the jungle, with its resolute men, its chance encounters, its not yet elapsed time, had taught me much more with respect to the very essence of my art, to the profound meaning of certain texts, to the ignored greatness of certain paths, than the reading of so many books that lie now, dead forever, in my library" (p. 263). He believes the jungle and the people in it have taught him the ideal of human existence. "Before the Commissioner I have realized that the maximum task presented to a human being is that of fabricating a destiny" (pp. 263–264). This becomes his overwhelming problem —to escape from the city and follow the path he has chosen. The city becomes a labyrinth. "The city doesn't let me go. Its streets wind around me like the cords of a weir, of a net, that had been thrown on me from above" (p. 266). His escape, however, is due not to any direct effort on his part but rather to the fortuitous sale of a piece of bad music.

For the second time the number seven appears; he has been away from Santa Mónica for seven months. With his wife the seventh day represented the unnatural nature of their marriage, the only time they could be husband and wife. With respect to the return to Santa Mónica it foreshadows the last, disastrous discovery he is to make, the opening of the seventh seal connected with the voyage. As he is about to take what he believes to be the final step in his return, he reflects, with fear, on the possibilities that remain behind him. "But then, already knowing that I pretend to admit that which I don't admit, a real fear assaults me: fear of everything I have just finished seeing, enduring, and having weigh on my existence. Fear of the tongs, fear of the executioner. I don't want to go back to writing bad music, knowing I'm writing bad music. I flee from useless occupations, from those who talk to deaden themselves, from empty days, from the gesture without meaning, and from the Apocalypse that sifts over all that" (p. 275). At this point his own apocalypse of disillusionment and demythification begins. He cannot find the passage leading to Santa Mónica. This is the first note of reality to enter into his relation to nature. He discovers he does not have the knowledge to directly confront the jungle; he needs a guide.

A reality more difficult to accept is forced upon him by Yannes, the miner, who destroys all the narrator's idealization and mythification of Rosario. "She no Penelope. Young woman, strong, beautiful, needs husband. She no Penelope. Nature woman here need man . . ." (p. 285). The possibility of paradise is gone, destroyed by a reality that in no way corresponds to the myth created by the narrator.

Thus the personal, individual nature of the voyage becomes clear. It was interior and emotional, not epic and transcendent. In retrospect the narrator comprehends his true relation to the people he had idealized. "The truth, the crushing truth—I understand it now—is that the people of those distant regions never believed in me. I was a loaned being. Rosario herself must have seen me as a Visitor . . ." (p. 285). He realizes how useless he was at Santa Mónica, where the only thing he could do—write music —was not understood and had no value. He was alienated there and did not know it.

His true and final loss of alienation is thus due to the process that began in Santa Mónica, the discovery of his artistic self, a self that at last he realizes cannot be separated from its epoch. The miracle of an escape from time is not for him. "But none of this is destined for me, because the only human race prohibited from freeing itself from the bonds of dates is the race of those who make art" (p. 286). The price he has paid for this knowledge is the loss of orientation in his epoch.

Thus his final position in terms of overall alienation is complex. Looking inward he has discovered his true self. Looking outward, at a philosophical level, he knows what his relation to his time must be, and he knows it springs from his essential self. But the direction his life will take and the control he will have over it are in doubt. It is possible that he will again be subject to the alienation caused by society, despite his knowledge of self. "I don't yet know whether I will be struck deaf and dumb by the blows of the Slave Master who someplace awaits me" (p. 286).

Carpentier covers a great deal of territory in his presentation of alienation. He first examines the alienating effects of modern society. Then he shows the artist's special relation to an alienating society and the posture this relation forces the artist to assume in respect to his own art. Cultural alienation is seen on several levels. The most important is the loss of alienation due to the protagonist's renewal of contact with the more vital culture of Latin

America, which was also that of his youth, so that it represents an encounter with formative influences of his personality. In his contact with more primitive cultures he is able to establish a feeling of being related to them by coincidence of activities. The origin of his artistic self is found through his discovery of the beginnings of music in a primitive tribe.

Alienation from nature is also of great importance. Renewed contact with Latin American nature in all its moods is one of the forces that counteracts the alienation induced by the artificiality of the city.

In Carpentier's novel, unlike those of the other authors studied, the presentation of the theme does not affect the structure of the novel or the imagery. The structure is determined by the content, the narrative of a journey. The divisions of the novel correspond to stages of the journey. Mythological references and associations are used to give meaning to the different stages but, in the last analysis, are seen to be adjuncts to the dominant theme, that of the artist in his relation to his epoch. The protagonist is seen to be essentially antiheroic, and this feature alone is enough to make it impossible to attribute any mythic stature to his being or his actions. Thus the relation of myth to alienation seen in the novel is that myth is used to provide an external dimension in the presentation of the theme of alienation. It has no effect on the form or development of the theme itself.

Alienation is presented in relation to generalized issues: social, cultural, and artistic alienation. Alienation caused by personality is not present. In comparison with Bombal's and Onetti's works, this is the unique aspect of Carpentier's achievement.

5. Concluding Remarks

The emphasis in this study has been on how alienation appeared and how it was used within the works examined, rather than on what it was. Various authors were relied upon for the definition of alienation and for their opinion of its meaning and importance.

The literary aspects were dealt with in the chapters on each of the writers studied. Bombal was seen to have a poetic approach to the theme. Onetti was shown to employ a fragmented imagery to convey the schizophrenic, or schizoid, extreme of alienation. Carpentier presented the socioeconomic aspects stressed by the writers on alienation whose views were presented in the first chapter. In addition he related alienation to the artist in modern society and used a myth as an adjunct in his manipulation of the theme.

When the authors are viewed together, however, there are several points not appearing in the separate discussions that merit further examination. These concern the meaning of the literary experience of alienation.

Erich Kahler saw alienation, due to conditions of modern life, leading to a feeling of nothingness, to a disgust for life. In the novels of two of the authors studied, María Luisa Bombal and

Juan Carlos Onetti, the main characters have this feeling as the center of their life experience. In neither case is it possible to say that it is caused by the conditions of modern life.

La última niebla takes place in no definite time and does not explore contemporary society. The protagonist's loss of self and retreat into fantasy are due mainly to conditions unique to her personal existence. That her encounter with an imaginary lover takes place in the city and that there is a city-country opposition maintained throughout the book are in no way related to her progression deeper into alienation. The country reinforces her natural bent toward solitude, and the city brings her in contact with people. The source of her alienation is within her.

Eladio Linacero, in *El pozo*, lives in a modern city and his experience of disgust and nothingness is heightened by his total solitude in the crowd. But the origin of his extreme alienation is found in self-hate, not in his reaction to modern life. The woman in *Tan triste como ella* is driven to suicide by the failure of her personal life. Brausen is put in relation to the alienation caused by socioeconomic conditions, but this alienation only reinforces his loss of self, a process that again has its roots in his personality. The town that has the most effect on Onetti's characters—and that in many ways does cause some of their alienation—is Santa María. But it is not modern. The alienating forces seen there are those of a traditional provincial small town.

Only the protagonist in *Los pasos perdidos* suffers the loss of self caused by modern society. When his social conditions change, so does his alienation. Of all the characters studied he is the least affected by his alienation. His artistic self, the center of his being, was never destroyed and only needed the proper conditions to emerge.

The least degree of alienation and loss of self seen results from purely social and economic conditions. The suffering and nothingness in the works of Onetti and Bombal are not due to these conditions. Neither are they due to any philosophical stance on the part of the characters. These two authors are dealing with a human experience rooted in the individual beings of their protagonists. This experience is not rigidly connected to time or place. Fritz Pappenheim in *The Alienation of Modern Man,* while concentrating on the socioeconomic alienation described by Marx, admits a wider interpretation but relates it to modern conditions: "The awareness that man in all stages of history has undergone some form and degree of alienation, and that this will be his fate also in the future, does not take from him the obligation to struggle against those forms of alienation which he meets today."[1]

Considered together, the writers studied have also taken a broad view of alienation. They have extended it far beyond socioeconomic boundaries, and in creating literature from the theme they have defined a mode of human experience.

NOTES

1. GENERAL ASPECTS OF ALIENATION

1. Fritz Pappenheim, *The Alienation of Modern Man*, p. 83.

2. Karl Marx, *Economic and Philosophic Manuscripts of 1844*, p. 66. All subsequent page references will be to this edition and will be cited in the text.

3. Herbert Read, *Art and Alienation*.

4. Gerald Sykes, *Alienation*.

5. Erich Fromm, *The Sane Society*, p. 111. All subsequent page references will be to this edition and will be cited in the text.

6. R. D. Laing, *The Politics of Experience*, p. 28.

7. Ibid., p. 17.

8. Albert Camus, *The Myth of Sisyphus and Other Essays*, p. 5.

9. Erich Kahler, *The Tower and the Abyss*, p. 185. All subsequent page references will be to this edition and will be cited in the text.

10. Pappenheim, *Alienation*, p. 66.

11. Anton Ehrenzweig, *The Hidden Order of Art*, p. 122.

2. MARÍA LUISA BOMBAL: ALIENATION AND THE POETIC IMAGE

1. María Luisa Bombal was born in Viña del Mar, Chile, on the eighth of June, 1910. Upon the death of her father she, her two sisters, and her mother went to Paris, where she studied at Notre Dame de l'Assomption. She had studied before at the school of Franciscan nuns at Viña del Mar. She graduated from the Sorbonne with a degree in philosophy and letters. She also studied drama in the school of Charles Dullin, director of the Théâtre Atelier in Paris. When she returned to Chile in 1931 she was active in theater, participating in a company directed by Luis Pizarro Espoz.

Bombal moved to Buenos Aires in 1933. In 1939 she made a short trip to the United States, where she made contact with William Faulkner, Sherwood Anderson, and Erskine Caldwell. After the trip she returned to Buenos Aires and resumed her job with the magazine *Sur*. A brief return to Chile in 1941 was followed by another trip to North America.

She married in 1944 and has one daughter. She now resides in New York and has published versions of her novels in English. In 1961 she returned briefly to Santiago. In 1963 she was reported to be working on another novel.

All of the foregoing information was taken from the introduction to *El árbol* in *Antología del cuento chileno*, pp. 433–436.

2. Cedomil Goić, *La novela chilena: Los mitos degradados*, p. 149. My translation.

3. María Luisa Bombal, *La última niebla*, p. 14. My translation. All subsequent references will be to this edition with page numbers given in the text.

4. Goić, *Novela chilena*, p. 144.

5. María Luisa Bombal, *La amortajada*, p. 99. My translation.

6. Margaret V. Campbell, "The Vaporous World of María Luisa Bombal," *Hispania* 44, no. 3 (September 1961), p. 415.

7. R. D. Laing, *The Divided Self*, p. 69.

8. Goić, *Novela chilena*, p. 156.

9. Ibid.

10. Joseph Gabel, *La fausse conscience*, p. 152. My translation.

11. Anton Ehrenzweig, *The Hidden Order of Art*, p. 14.

12. Laing, *Divided Self*, p. 138.

13. Ibid., p. 17.

3. JUAN CARLOS ONETTI: ALIENATION AND THE FRAGMENTED IMAGE

1. Juan Carlos Onetti was born in Montevideo in 1909. There is little information available about his life or family. Luis Harss and Barbara Dohmann in *Into the Mainstream*, p. 182, say:

We find out little about Onetti's early years. After high school, when he was about twenty years old, he moved to Buenos Aires, the promised land, where he took random courses in the university and held innumerable odd jobs—which he refuses to name, bored or ashamed of them—before eventually making a career of journalism. He was with Reuter's News Service, became their Buenos Aires bureau chief in the early forties. At the same time he was associated with and helped edit *Marcha* in Montevideo. After Reuter's, he was the editor in chief—up to about 1950—of an Argentine magazine, *Vea y Lea*. Then he was in charge of a publicity magazine called *Impetu*.

According to Harss and Dohmann, Onetti remained in Buenos Aires until 1954, when he returned to Montevideo. Following the triumph of Luis Batlle Berres, Onetti moved into politics, taking over the party paper, *Acción*. He remained with the paper for several years, until he moved to a library job with the Institute of Arts and Letters, which he was holding at the time of his interview with Harss and Dohmann.

2. Angel Rama, "Origen de un novelista de una generación literaria," introduction to *El pozo*, p. 49. My translation.

3. The dates are taken from Caracé Hernández, "Juan Carlos Onetti: Pistas para sus laberintos," *Mundo Nuevo* 34 (April 1969): 71–72.

4. Ibid.

5. Mario Benedetti, "Juan Carlos Onetti y la aventura del hombre," in *Literatura uruguaya del siglo XX*, pp. 79–80. My translation.

6. Emir Rodríguez Monegal, "La fortuna de Onetti," in *Literatura uruguaya del medio siglo*, pp. 241–242. My translation.

7. Harss and Dohmann, *Mainstream*, p. 181.

8. See Rodríguez Monegal, "La fortuna de Onetti," p. 222.

9. Harss and Dohmann, *Mainstream*, p. 174.

10. Juan Carlos Onetti, *Juntacadáveres*, pp. 26–27. My translation.

11. Benedetti, "Juan Carlos Onetti," p. 76.

12. Harss and Dohmann, *Mainstream*, p. 177.

13. Ibid., p. 185.

14. Rama, "Origen," p. 54.

15. Juan Carlos Onetti, *El pozo*, in *Novelas cortas*, p. 7. My translation. Subsequent page references will be to this edition and will be cited in the text.

16. Rama, "Origen," p. 82.

17. Ibid., p. 86.

18. See Anton Ehrenzweig, *The Hidden Order of Art*, p. 122; see also the discussion of the process in relation to *La última niebla*, pp. 34–35 in this study.

19. Emir Rodríguez Monegal, "Juan Carlos Onetti y la novela rioplatense," *Número* 3, nos. 13–14 (March–June 1951): 175–188.

20. Benedetti, "Juan Carlos Onetti," p. 77.

21. Rodríguez Monegal, "La fortuna de Onetti," p. 223. My translation.

22. Juan Carlos Onetti, *Tan triste como ella*, in *Novelas cortas*, p. 135. My translation. Subsequent page references will be to this edition and will be cited in the text.

23. Juan Carlos Onetti, *La vida breve*, p. 53. My translation. All subsequent page references will be to this edition and will be cited in the text.

24. R. D. Laing, *The Divided Self*, p. 17.

25. Juan Carlos Onetti, *El astillero*, p. 87. My translation. All subsequent page references will be to this edition and will be cited in the text.

4. ALEJO CARPENTIER: ALIENATION, CULTURE, AND MYTH

1. Alejo Carpentier was born in Cuba in 1904, of immigrant parents. His father was French and his mother of Russian origin. French was the language of his home. He received his primary education in Cuba, and some of his secondary studies were done in France, the rest completed in Cuba. He began his university career, which he did not finish, in Cuba, studying architecture and then music. He left the university to go to France, where he continued his study of music. Returning to Cuba he became a journalist, writing articles of musical and theatrical criticism. In 1927 he was jailed in

Cuba for having signed a proclamation against Machado. In jail he wrote his first novel, *Ecue-Yamba-O*. He was released in 1928 and went to France, to remain for eleven years. In 1939 he returned to Havana and was named director of radio broadcasting for the Ministry of Education. He moved to Caracas in 1945, to start a radio station, and remained there for fourteen years. Carpentier returned to Cuba in 1959 and became executive director of the Editorial Nacional de Cuba. He now lives in Paris, as the cultural attaché of the Cuban Embassy.

2. Klaus Müller-Bergh, "Alejo Carpentier: Autor y obra en su época," *Revista Iberoamericana* 33, no. 63 (1967): 15. My translation.

3. Angel Flores, "Magical Realism in Spanish American Fiction," *Hispania* 39, no. 2 (May 1955): 187–192.

4. Carlos Santander, "Lo maravilloso en la obra de Alejo Carpentier," *Atenea* 42, no. 159 (1965): 101. My translation.

5. Alejo Carpentier, *Tientos y diferencias*, p. 37. My translation.

6. Ibid., p. 36.

7. Santander, "Lo maravilloso," p. 102.

8. Julieta Campos, *La imagen en el espejo*, p. 131. My translation.

9. Santander, "Lo maravilloso," p. 102.

10. Salvador Bueno, *La letra como testigo*, p. 173. My translation.

11. Alejo Carpentier, *Los pasos perdidos*, p. 11. My translation. All subsequent references will be to this edition and will be cited in the text.

12. Juan Loveluck, "*Los pasos perdidos*: Jasón y el nuevo vellocino," *Cuadernos Hispanoamericanos* 55, no. 165 (September 1963): 419. My translation.

13. Klaus Müller-Bergh, "Reflexiones sobre los mitos en Alejo Carpentier," *Insula* 23, nos. 260–261 (July–August 1968): 22. My translation.

14. Joseph Campbell, *The Hero with a Thousand Faces*, p. 30.

15. Bueno, *La letra*, p. 174.

16. Javier Martínez-Palacio, "Los anti-héroes de Alejo Carpentier," *Insula* 20, no. 226 (September 1965): 1. My translation.

17. Ibid., p. 14.

18. Müller-Bergh, "Reflexiones," p. 22.

5. CONCLUDING REMARKS

1. Fritz Pappenheim, *The Alienation of Modern Man*, p. 115.

SELECTED BIBLIOGRAPHY

GENERAL SOURCES

Barret, William. *Irrational Man: A Study in Existential Philosophy.* Garden City: Anchor Books, 1962.

――――. *What Is Existentialism?* New York: Grove Press, 1964.

Campbell, Joseph. *The Hero with a Thousand Faces.* New York: Pantheon Books, 1949.

Camus, Albert. *The Myth of Sisyphus and Other Essays.* New York: Vintage Books, 1955.

Caute, David. *Essential Writings of Karl Marx.* New York: Macmillan, 1967.

Ehrenzweig, Anton. *The Hidden Order of Art.* Berkeley: University of California Press, 1967.

Franco, Jean. *The Modern Culture of Latin America: Society and the Artist.* Middlesex: Penguin Books, 1970.

Fromm, Erich. *Man for Himself: An Inquiry into the Psychology of Ethics.* New York: Fawcett World Library, 1969.

――――. *The Sane Society.* New York: Fawcett World Library, 1970.

Gabel, Joseph. *La fausse conscience.* Paris: Editions de minuit, 1962.

Harss, Luis, and Barbara Dohmann. *Into the Mainstream: Conversations with Latin-American Writers.* New York: Harper & Row, 1967.

Kahler, Erich. *The Tower and the Abyss: An Inquiry into the Transformation of Man.* New York: Viking Press, 1967.

Laing, R. D. *The Divided Self.* Middlesex: Penguin Books, 1965.

———. *The Politics of Experience*. New York: Ballantine Books, 1967.

Marx, Karl. *Economic and Philosophic Manuscripts of 1844*. Moscow: Progress Publishers, 1967.

Pappenheim, Fritz. *The Alienation of Modern Man: An Interpretation Based on Marx and Tönnies*. New York: Monthly Review Press, 1967.

Read, Herbert. *Art and Alienation*. New York: Horizon Press, 1967.

Sykes, Gerald. *Alienation*. 2 vols. New York: Braziller, 1964.

Sypher, Wylie. *Literature and Technology: The Alien Vision*. New York: Vintage Books, 1971.

———. *Loss of Self in Modern Literature and Art*. New York: Vintage Books, 1962.

MARÍA LUISA BOMBAL
Works by Bombal

Bombal, María Luisa. "Historia de María Griselda." *Sur*, no. 142 (August 1946), pp. 41–63.

———. *La amortajada*. 1st. ed. Buenos Aires: Ediciones Sur, 1938.

———. *La amortajada*. 4th. ed. Buenos Aires: Editorial Andina, 1968.

———. "Las trenzas." *Saber Vivir* 2 (September 1940): 36–37.

———. *La última niebla*. 3d. ed. Santiago: Nascimento, 1962.

———. "Mar, cielo y tierra." *Saber Vivir* 1 (August 1940): 34, 35.

Works about Bombal

Allen, Marta E. "Dos estilos de novela: Marta Brunet y María Luisa Bombal." *Revista Iberoamericana* 35 (1952): 63–91.

Alonso, Amado. "Aparición de una novelista." Introduction to *La última niebla*, pp. 7–34. 3d. ed. Santiago: Nascimento, 1962.

Borges, Jorge Luis. "*La amortajada*." *Sur*, no. 47 (August 1938), pp. 80–81.

Brown, Catherine Meredith. "Haunted Hacienda." *Saturday Review of Literature*, 3 May 1947, p. 22.

Campbell, Margaret V. "The Vaporous World of María Luisa Bombal." *Hispania* 44, no. 3 (September 1961): 415–419.

Correa, Carlos René. "María Luisa Bombal." *Atenea* 199 (1942): 17–22.

Goić, Cedomil. *La novela chilena: Los mitos degradados*. Santiago: Editorial Universitaria, 1968.

———. "*La última niebla*: Consideraciones en torno a la estructura de la novela contemporánea." *Anales de la Universidad de Chile* 128 (1963): 59–83.

"María Luisa Bombal." In *Antología del cuento chileno*, pp. 433–436. Santiago: Instituto de Literatura Chilena, 1963.

Silva Castro, Raúl. *Panorama de la novela chilena*. Mexico City: Fondo de Cultura Económica, 1955.

———. *Panorama literario de Chile*. Santiago: Editorial Universitaria, 1961.

Torres-Ríoseco, Arturo. "El estilo en las novelas de María Luisa Bombal." In *Ensayos sobre literatura latinoamericana*, pp. 179–190. 2d. series. Berkeley: University of California Press, 1958.

JUAN CARLOS ONETTI
Works by Onetti

Onetti, Juan Carlos. *Cuentos completos*. Buenos Aires: Centro Editor de América Latina, 1967.

———. *El astillero*. Buenos Aires: Compañía General Fabril Editora, 1969.

———. *Juntacadáveres*. 2d. ed. Montevideo: Editorial Alfa, 1966.

———. *La vida breve*. Buenos Aires: Editorial Sudamericana, Col. Indice, 1968.

———. *Novelas cortas*. [*El pozo, Los adioses, La cara de la desgracia, Tan triste como ella*, and *Para una tumba sin nombre*.] Caracas: Monte Avila, 1968.

———. *Para esta noche*. 3d. ed. Montevideo: Bolsilibros Arca, 1967.

———. *Tierra de nadie*. 3d. ed. Montevideo: Ediciones de la Banda Oriental, 1968.

Works about Onetti

Ainsa, Fernando. *Las trampas de Onetti*. Montevideo: Editorial Alfa, 1970.

———. "Onetti: Un 'outsider' resignado." *Cuadernos Hispanoamericanos* 81, no. 243 (March 1970): 612–638.

Benedetti, Mario. "Juan Carlos Onetti y la aventura del hombre." In *Literatura uruguaya del siglo XX*, pp. 76–95. Montevideo: Editorial Alfa, 1963.

Bueno, Salvador. "*Juntacadáveres*: ¿novela social?" *Indice*, 1 February 1971 and 15 February 1971, pp. 61–62.

Concha, Jaime. "Un tema de Juan Carlos Onetti." *Revista Iberoamericana* 35 (1969): 351–363.

Cresta de Leguizamón, María Luisa. "Una novela uruguaya." *Libros Selectos* 24 (1965): 13–20.

Gilio, María Ester. "Onetti y sus demonios interiores." *Marcha*, 1 July 1966, pp. 25–26.

Grande, Félix. "Juan Carlos Onetti, y una escenografía de obsesiones." *Cuadernos Hispanoamericanos* 78, no. 234 (June 1969): 710–722.

Harss, Luis. "Juan Carlos Onetti, o las sombras en la pared." In *Los nuestros*, pp. 214–251. Buenos Aires: Editorial Sudamericana, 1966.

Harss, Luis, and Barbara Dohmann. *Into the Mainstream: Conversations with Latin-American Writers*. New York: Harper & Row, 1967.

Hernández, Caracé. "Juan Carlos Onetti: Pistas para sus laberintos." *Mundo Nuevo* 34 (April 1969): 65–72.

Maggi, Carlos. *Gardel, Onetti, y algo más*. Montevideo: Editorial Alfa, 1967.

———. "Retrato de Juan Carlos Onetti." *Marcha*, 11 August 1961, p. 28.

Mercier, Lucién. "Juan Carlos Onetti en busca del infierno." *Marcha*, 19 October 1962, pp. 30–31.

Rama, Angel. "Origen de un novelista y de una generación literaria." Introduction to *El pozo*, pp. 49–100. Montevideo: Bolsilibros Arca, 1967.

Rodríguez Monegal, Emir. "Juan Carlos Onetti y la novela rioplatense." *Número* 3, nos. 13–14 (March–June 1951): 175–188.

———. "Juan Carlos Onetti y la novela rioplatense." In *Narradores de esta América*. Montevideo: Editorial Alfa, n.d. [Same article as in *Número*.]

———. "La fortuna de Onetti." In *Literatura uruguaya del medio siglo*, pp. 221–260. Montevideo: Editorial Alfa, 1966.

Verani, Hugo J. "En torno a *Los adioses* de Juan Carlos Onetti." *Anales de la Universidad de Chile* 124, no. 145 (January–March 1968): 35–57.

ALEJO CARPENTIER
Works by Carpentier

Carpentier, Alejo. "Autobiografía de urgencia." *Insula* 20, no. 218 (January 1965): 3.

———. *Ecue-Yamba-O*. Buenos Aires: Editorial Xanadu, 1968.

———. *El reino de este mundo*. 3d. ed. Montevideo: Bolsilibros Arca, 1968.

————. *El siglo de las luces.* 2d. ed. Havana: Ediciones Revolución, 1965.

————. *Guerra del tiempo.* ["El camino de Santiago," "Viaje a la semilla," "Semejante a la noche," and *El acoso.*] 4th. ed. Mexico City: Compañía General de Ediciones, 1967.

————. *Los pasos perdidos.* 6th. ed. Mexico City: Compañía General de Ediciones, 1968.

————. *Tientos y diferencias.* 2d. ed. Montevideo: Bolsilibros Arca, 1970.

Works about Carpentier

Alegría, Fernando. "Alejo Carpentier: Realismo mágico." *Humanitas* 1 (1960): 345–372.

————. *Historia de la novela hispanoamericana.* 3d. ed. Mexico City: Ediciones de Andrea, 1966.

Bueno, Salvador. "Alejo Carpentier, novelista antillano y universal." In *La letra como testigo,* pp. 153–179. Santa Clara, Cuba: Universidad Central de las Villas, 1957.

Campos, Jorge. "La antilla de Alejo Carpentier." *Insula* 21, no. 240 (November 1966): 11, 15.

Campos, Julieta. "El realismo subjetivo de Alejo Carpentier." *Revista de la Universidad de México* 13, no. 11 (July 1959): 17–20.

————. "Realidad y fantasía de Alejo Carpentier" and "Carpentier: El estilo de nuestro mundo." In *La imagen en el espejo,* pp. 127–140. Mexico City: Universidad Nacional, 1965.

Coddou, Marcelo. " 'El reino de este mundo.' " *Atenea* 166, no. 417 (July–September 1967): 9–11.

Donahue, Francis. "Alejo Carpentier: La preocupación del tiempo." *Cuadernos Hispanoamericanos* 68, no. 202 (October 1966): 133–151.

Dorfman, Ariel. "El reino de este Carpentier." *Ercilla,* 19 July 1967, p. 28.

————. "El sentido de la historia en la obra de Alejo Carpentier." In *Imaginación y violencia en América,* pp. 93–137. Santiago: Editorial Universitaria, 1970.

————. "La libertad y la guillotina." *Ercilla,* 6 October 1965, p. 32.

Dumas, Claude. "*El siglo de las luces* de Alejo Carpentier, novela filosófica." *Cuadernos Americanos* 25, no. 147 (July–August 1966): 187–210.

Fell, Claude. "Rencontre avec Alejo Carpentier." *Les Langues Modernes* 59 (May–June 1965): 101–109.

Fisher, Sofía. "Notas sobre el tiempo en Alejo Carpentier." *Insula* 23, nos. 260–261 (July–August 1968): 5, 8.

Flores, Angel. "Magical Realism in Spanish American Fiction." *Hispania* 39, no. 2 (May 1955): 187–192.

Giacoman, Helmy F. "La estructura musical en la novelística de Alejo Carpentier." *Hispanofila* 11, no. 33 (May 1968): 49–57.

———. "La relación músico-literaria entre la tercera sinfonía 'Eroica' de Beethoven y la novela *El acoso* de Alejo Carpentier." *Cuadernos Americanos* 27, no. 158 (May–June 1968): 113–129.

Glissant, Eduard. "Alejo Carpentier et 'l'autre Amérique.'" *Critique* 12, no. 105 (February 1966): 113–119.

Harss, Luis, and Barbara Dohmann. "Alejo Carpentier, or the eternal return." In *Into the Mainstream: Conversations with Latin American Writers*, pp. 37–67. New York: Harper & Row, 1967.

Hodoušek, Eduard. "Eininge Bemerkungen zur Personlichkeit und zum literarischen Schaffen von Alejo Carpentier." *Wissenschaftliche Zeitschrift der Universität Rostock* 14 (1965): 41–47.

Lastra, Pedro. "Notas sobre la narrativa de Alejo Carpentier." *Anales de la Universidad de Chile* 120, no. 125 (1965): 94–101.

Leante, César. "Confesiones sencillas de un escritor barroco." *Cuba, Revista Mensual* 3, no. 24 (April 1964): 30–33.

Loveluck, Juan. "*Los pasos perdidos*: Jasón y el nuevo vellocino." *Cuadernos Hispanoamericanos* 55, no. 165 (September 1963): 414–426.

Martínez-Palacio, Javier. "Los anti-héroes de Alejo Carpentier." *Insula* 20, no. 226 (September 1965): 1, 14.

Müller-Bergh, Klaus. "Alejo Carpentier: Autor y obra en su época." *Revista Iberoamericana* 33, no. 63 (1967): 9–43.

———. "En torno al estilo de Alejo Carpentier en *Los pasos perdidos*." *Cuadernos Hispanoamericanos* 73, no. 219 (March 1968): 554–569.

———. "Reflexiones sobre los mitos en Alejo Carpentier." *Insula* 23, nos. 260–261 (July–August 1968): 5, 22–23.

Pérez Minik, Domingo. "La guillotina de Alejo Carpentier: En torno a *El siglo de las luces*." *Insula* 21, no. 238 (September 1966): 3.

Rama, Angel. "Coronación de Carpentier." *Marcha*, 22 May 1964, pp. 1, 4.

———. "Las novelas de lo maravilloso." *Marcha*, 17 August 1962, pp. 30–31.

———. "Una revolución frustrada." *Marcha*, 29 May 1964, pp. 29–30.

Rodríguez Alcalá, Hugo. "Sentido de 'El camino de Santiago' de Alejo Carpentier." *Humanitas* 5 (1964): 245–254.

Rodríguez Monegal, Emir. "Dos novelas de Alejo Carpentier." In *Narradores de esta América*, pp. 270–287. Montevideo: Editorial Alfa, n.d.

Santander T., Carlos. "Lo maravilloso en la obra de Alejo Carpentier." *Atenea* 42, no. 159 (1965): 99–126.

Sorel Martínez, Andrés. "El mundo novelístico de Alejo Carpentier." *Cuadernos Hispanoamericanos* 61, no. 182 (February 1965): 304–320.

Vargas Llosa, Mario. "Cuatro preguntas a Alejo Carpentier." *Marcha*, 12 March 1965, pp. 31–32.

Verzasconi, Ray. "Juan and Sisyphus in Carpentier's 'El camino de Santiago.'" *Hispania* 48, no. 1 (March 1965): 70–75.

Weber, Frances Wyers. "*El acoso*: Alejo Carpentier's War on Time." *PMLA* 78 (1963): 440–448.

INDEX

abstractification: and alienation, 6–7

accessory: structural role of, 19

El acoso (Carpentier), 81

action: habitual vs. meaningless, 44–45; repetition in, 84–85

Los adioses (Onetti), 37, 44

alienation: existential interpretation of, 5, 9–13; and internal personal forces, 15; literary interpretation of, 13–14, 107–109; and literary structure, 15–16; manipulation of, 77–79, 80; vs. "marvelous reality," 82; multifaceted nature of, 104–105; socioeconomic interpretation of, 3–9

Alienation (Sykes), 5

The Alienation of Modern Man (Pappenheim), 3, 10; historical perspective of, 109

Alonso, Amado: on mist as leitmotiv, 23; on *La última niebla*, 16, 19–20; on use of external elements, 19

La amortajada (Bombal), 15, 17, 18

anonymity: and alienation, 7

"Los anti-héroes de Alejo Carpentier" (Martínez-Palacio), 99

archetypes: and human relations, 96–97

Arlt, Roberto, 39

art: and discovery of self, 101, 104; vs. nature, 93–94; and process of alienation, 12; schizophrenia in, 13–14

Art and Alienation (Read), 5

artist: alienation of, 86–87

El astillero (Onetti), 37, 56, 72; ambiguous ending of, 79; ambiguous narrator of, 79–80; heroism in, 77–78; manipulation of alienation in, 77–79, 80; relative optimism of, 64; repeated action in, 44

baroque prose: suitability of, for Latin American novels, 82–83

Benedetti, Mario: on alienation in Onetti's work, 39–40; on Onetti "cycle," 56; on Onetti short story vs. Onetti novel, 38

biblical motifs, 85–86; South American adaptation of, 93

body, human: relation of, to self, 20–23; separation of, from self, 26–27

Bombal, María Luisa, 3, 13, 14; biographical sketch of, 110–111;

and postsurrealist "new sensibility," 16; presentation of alienation by, 107–108; use of external elements by, 19. Works: *La amortajada*, 15, 17, 18; *El Canciller*, 15; *The Foreign Minister*, 15; *The House of Mist*, 15, 18; "Islas nuevas," 18; *La última niebla*, 15–16, 17–21, 22–34, 35

Bueno, Salvador, 83, 94; on use of counterpoint, 91

Campbell, Joseph: *The Hero with a Thousand Faces* by, 90
Campbell, Margaret: on Bombal's theme, 18
Campos, Julieta: on myth in *Los pasos perdidos*, 83
Camus, Albert: on alienation, 10
El Canciller (Bombal), 15
capitalism: and alienation, 6–7
La cara de la desgracia (Onetti), 44, 47
Carpentier, Alejo, 3, 14; on aspects of alienation, 83; on baroque prose, 82–83; biographical sketch of, 112–113; early literary interests of, 81–82; on "marvelous reality," 82; presentation of alienation by, 108. Works: *El acoso*, 81; *Ecue-Yamba-O*, 81; *La música en Cuba*, 81; *Los pasos perdidos*, 81, 82, 83–105; *El reino de este mundo*, 81; *El siglo de las luces*, 81; *Tientos y diferencias*, 82; "Viaje a la semilla," 81
Celine, Louis-Ferdinand, 39
city: as alienating environment, 84–85, 86; rhythms of, 102; sickness of, 102, 103; as symbolic/structural device, 18–19. See also village
collective: vs. community, 10–11
community: vs. collective, 10–11
country: as symbolic/structural device, 18–19

Cuentos completos (Onetti), 38

death: vs. love, 25–26
description. See accessory
disillusionment: as medium of existence, 64–65
The Divided Self (Laing), 3; treatment of body-self relationship in, 21–22
Dohmann, Barbara: on alienation in Onetti's work, 40; on Onetti's use of fact and falsehood, 39
Dos Passos, John, 39
dreams: and emotional life, 46; vs. mist, 23; and rational/irrational levels of alienation, 60–61; vs. reality, 47–53. See also fantasy

Ecue-Yamba-O (Carpentier), 81
Ehrenzweig, Anton: on schizoid vision, 34–35; on schizophrenic art, 14
environment: and cultural alienation, 92–93
evasion: as life-giving force, 71–72
existentialism: concept of alienation in, 9–13
experience, primary: necessity of, 32–33

fantasy: and loss of self, 28, 29. See also dreams
Faulkner, William, 39
filth: emotional impact of, 42
Flores, Angel: on "magical realism," 82
The Foreign Minister (Bombal), 15
Freud, Sigmund: and principle of nonfrustration, 8
Fromm, Erich: on alienation/schizophrenia continuum, 35; concept of alienation of, 5–9, 86, 87; definition of alienation by, 5; on insanity, 8–9. Works: *Man for Himself*, 3, 7–8; *The Sane Society*, 3, 5–7, 8–9

Gabel, Joseph: on schizoid vision, 34
garden: as symbol for self, 63–64; as symbol for sexual conflict, 65–67
Gemeinschaft und Gesellschaft (Tönnies), 10
generalizations: personification of, 87–88
Goić, Cedomil: on postsurrealist "new sensibility," 16; on symbolic/structural function of mist, 23, 32; on *La última niebla*, 15, 16, 19

hair: as symbolic/structural device, 19–20
Harss, Luis: on alienation in Onetti's work, 40; on Onetti's use of fact and falsehood, 39
Hegel, Georg Wilhelm Friedrich: concept of alienation of, 12. Work: *The Phenomenology of the Mind*, 4
heroism: in face of alienation, 77–78; nature of, 89–90; negation of, in *Los pasos perdidos*, 95, 98–100
The Hero with a Thousand Faces (J. Campbell), 90
The House of Mist (Bombal), 15, 18

"El infierno tan temido" (Onetti), 38, 71; repetitive action in, 44–45
El infierno tan temido y otros cuentos (Onetti), 38
"Islas nuevas" (Bombal): presentation of love in, 18

"Jacob y el otro" (Onetti), 38
journey: as metaphor for alienation, 84, 85; mythical aspects of, 89–90; stages of, vs. stages in alienation, 88–89, 91–105
Jung, Carl, 12

jungle: idealization of, 102–103; symbolic significance of, 93, 96, 99
Juntacadáveres (Onetti), 37, 39, 71, 79–80

Kahler, Erich: on alienation/schizophrenia continuum, 35; on community/collective contrast, 10–11; concept of alienation of, 10–13, 14, 107. Work: *The Tower and the Abyss*, 3, 10–13

labor: alienating influence of, 4–5, 6–7, 73–74, 85, 86
Laing, R. D.: on body-self relation, 21–22; definition of alienation by, 5; on loss of self, 35; on schizoid personality, 9, 35, 75. Works: *The Divided Self*, 3; *The Politics of Experience*, 3
language: and cultural alienation, 91–92
Latin American novel: ideal of, 82–83
Leante, César, 83
letter (epistle): as literary device, 58–59
Literature and Technology: The Alien Vision (Sypher), 3
Loss of Self in Modern Literature and Art (Sypher), 3, 9
love: and body-self relation, 22–23; vs. death, 25–26; fantasizing of, 26–31; mutability of, 62; purity of, 52; in social context, 17–18
Loveluck, Juan, 84; on heroism in *Los pasos perdidos*, 89
lust: imagery of, 48, 49–50. See also sexuality

Man for Himself (Fromm), 3; and alienated man, 7–8
Martínez-Palacio, Javier: "Los anti-héroes de Alejo Carpentier" by, 99

"marvelous reality": definition of, 82

Marx, Karl, 6, 10, 11; concept of alienation of, 3–5, 9, 12, 14, 73, 86, 87, 109

mass man: alienation of, 72–73

men (sex specific): social function of, 17

mist: cumulative significance of, 33–34, 35; destruction of reality by, 21, 23–25; as representation of the ominous, 31–34; unreality created by, 25–31; and vision, 34–35

monomyth: explanation of, 90

Müller-Bergh, Klaus, 84; on function of myth in *Los pasos perdidos*, 100; on mythical references in *Los pasos perdidos*, 89–90

music: as expression of will, 88; as impetus to artistic rebirth, 100–101

La música en Cuba (Carpentier), 81

narrator: ambiguity of, 79–80; vs. author, 40; deception by, 45–47, 57–58

nature: vs. art, 93–94; vs. civilization, 95–96; as hostile force, 99; and self-discovery, 94, 95

La Nausée (Sartre), 13

novel: vs. short story, 38

—, Latin American: ideal of, 82–83

Onetti, Juan Carlos, 3, 13, 14; biographical sketch of, 111; presentation of alienation by, 39–40, 107–108; prose style of, 38–39; short stories vs. novels of, 38. Works: *Los adioses*, 37, 44; *El astillero*, 37, 44, 56, 64, 72, 77–80; *La cara de la desgracia*, 44, 47; *Cuentos completos*, 38; "El infierno tan temido," 38, 44–45, 71; *El infierno tan temido y otros*

cuentos, 38; "Jacob y el otro," 38; *Juntacadáveres*, 37, 39, 71, 79–80; *Para esta noche*, 37, 40, 45; *Para una tumba sin nombre*, 37, 44, 45, 47, 57–58; *El pozo*, 37, 38, 39, 40–44, 45–57, 58, 61, 62, 64, 67, 71, 72, 75; *Un sueño realizado y otros cuentos*, 38; *Tan triste como ella*, 44, 55, 56–72, 75; *Tierra de nadie*, 37, 39, 40, 45; *La vida breve*, 37, 39, 45, 56, 72–77, 78

Pappenheim, Fritz: on alienation through history, 109. Work: *The Alienation of Modern Man*, 3, 10, 109

Para esta noche (Onetti), 37, 40, 45

Para una tumba sin nombre (Onetti), 37, 44, 45, 47, 57–58

Los pasos perdidos (Carpentier), 81, 82; alienation of artist in, 86–87, 101, 104; antiheroic bias in, 95, 98–100; biblical motifs in, 85–86; capitalized generic terms in, 87–88, 97; city environment in, 84–85, 86, 102, 103; discovery of self in, 94, 95, 101, 104; heroism in, 89–90; journey metaphor in, 84, 85; jungle motif in, 93, 94, 96, 99, 101, 102–103; presentation of alienation in, 108; repetitive action in, 84–85; stages of journey in, vs. stages in alienation, 88–89, 91–105; treatment of nature in, 93–97, 99

The Phenomenology of the Mind (Hegel), 4

The Politics of Experience (Laing), 3

El pozo (Onetti), 37, 39, 56, 75; deceitful narrator in, 45–47, 54; dream vs. reality in, 47–53, 55–56; explores theme of literary creation, 40–42, 55; expression

of disillusionment in, 43–44, 50–51, 52, 53–54, 61, 64; fragmented vision of, 42, 48, 50, 51, 54–55; idea of purity in, 51–53; presentation of alienation in, 108; repeated action in, 53, 54; schizophrenia of, 55, 56, 71; symbolism of, 55; treatment of sexuality in, 48–50, 51–52, 55, 62, 67
Prometheus, 89
prostitute: purity of, 51–53
psychoanalysis: effect of, on art, 12
purity: of love, 52; of prostitute, 51–53

Rama, Angel: on dreams, 49, 51; on solitude, 40; on Uruguayan culture, 37
Read, Herbert: *Art and Alienation* by, 5
reality: and alienation, 8–9; vs. dreams, 47–53; vs. evolution of art and science, 12. *See also* "marvelous reality"; visual reality
El reino de este mundo (Carpentier), 81
Rodríguez Monegal, Emir: on Onetti "cycle," 56; on Onetti prose style, 38; on suicide imagery, 57

The Sane Society (Fromm), 3; presentation of alienation in, 5–7, 8–9
Santander, Carlos, 84; on creation symbol, 86; on heroism in *Los pasos perdidos*, 90; on "the marvelous," 82; on mythical geography, 83; on women as mythical representation, 96. Work: "Lo maravilloso en la obra de Alejo Carpentier," 82
Sartre, Jean Paul, 76; *La Nausée* by, 13

schizoid personality: definition of, 9, 35
schizophrenia: in art, 9, 13–14; literary use of, 40, 55, 56, 75–76
science: effect of, on view of reality, 12
self: destruction of, 63–64, 68–71, 76–77; discovery of, 30–33, 94, 95, 104; loss of, 8–9, 74–75; loss of, through fantasy, 28, 29; relation of, to human body, 20–23; separation of, from body, 26–27
sexuality: alienation from, 59–60, 61; and self-destruction, 68–71; symbolized by garden, 65–67. *See also* lust
Shelley, Percy Bysshe, 91
short story: vs. novel, 38
El siglo de las luces (Carpentier), 81
solitude: vs. communication, 40–41; and disillusionment, 43–44
Un sueño realizado y otros cuentos (Onetti), 38
suffering: alienating influence of, 62–63
surrealist movement, 81–82
Sykes, Gerald: *Alienation* by, 5
Sypher, Wylie: *Literature and Technology: The Alien Vision* by, 3; *Loss of Self in Modern Literature and Art* by, 3, 9

Tan triste como ella (Onetti), 44, 55, 75; deceitful narrator in, 57–58; dream imagery in, 60–61; expression of disillusionment in, 64–65, 71–72; introductory letter in, 58–59; presentation of alienation in, 108; ritual suicide in, 70–71; sexual alienation in, 59–60, 61, 68–70, 71; sexual obsession in, 57, 65–68; significance of plot to, 57; symbolism of, 56, 63–64, 65–67, 69–71; treatment of suffering in, 62–63

Tientos y differencias (Carpentier), 82

Tierra de nadie (Onetti), 37, 39, 40, 45

Tönnies, Ferdinand: *Gemeinschaft und Gesellschaft* by, 10

The Tower and the Abyss (Kahler), 3; presentation of alienation in, 10–13

town. *See* city

travel. *See* journey

La última niebla (Bombal): city-country dichotomy in, 18–19; literary structure of, 15–16; presentation of alienation in, 15, 16, 108; structural use of accessory in, 19–20; symbolic/structural use of mist in, 23–34, 35; treatment of body/self relation in, 20–23; on women in society, 16–18

Ulysses, 89

vanguardist movement, 81

"Viaje a la semilla" (Carpentier), 81

La vida breve (Onetti), 37, 56, 71, 78; ambiguous narrator in, 45; destruction of self in, 76–77; fictional geography of, 39, 75; loss of self in, 74–75; schizoid experience in, 75–76; social alienation in, 72–74; theme of creation in, 75, 76, 77

village: nonalienating influence of, 92–93

vision: aberrations in, 34–35; fragmentation of, 42, 48, 50, 51, 54–55

visual reality: distortion of, 23–24

women: as archetypal representations, 96–97; and disillusionment of alienated man, 50–51, 52; loss of innocence by, 62; position of, in society, 16–18

worker: alienation of, 4–5, 6–7